THE TRUTH
ABOUT WORLDVIEWS

**Other Evangelical Training Association
books from Crossway Books**

BIBLICAL ESSENTIALS

THE TRUTH ABOUT WORLDVIEWS

A Biblical Understanding of
Worldview Alternatives

JAMES P. ECKMAN

CROSSWAY BOOKS

A DIVISION OF
GOOD NEWS PUBLISHERS
WHEATON, ILLINOIS

The Truth About Worldviews

Copyright © 2004 by Evangelical Training Association

Published by Crossway Books
        a division of Good News Publishers
        1300 Crescent Street
        Wheaton, Illinois 60187

Cover design: Josh Dennis

Cover photo: Adobe Image Library

First printing 2004

Printed in the United States of America

Scripture quotations are taken from the *New American Standard Bible*® Copyright © The Lockman Foundation 1960, 1962, 1963, 1968, 1971, 1972, 1973, 1975, 1977. Used by permission. (www.Lockman.org)

Library of Congress Cataloging-in-Publication Data
Eckman, James P. (James Paul)
   The truth about worldviews : a biblical understanding of worldview
alternatives / James P. Eckman.
     p. cm. (Biblical essentials series)
   Includes bibliographical references.
   ISBN 1-58134-672-7 (pbk.)
   1. Religions. 2. Apologetics. 3. Christianity—Philosophy. I. Title.
II. Series.
BL80.3.E35   2004
239—dc22   2004015838

VP		13	12	11	10	09	08	07	06	05	04
15	14	13	12	11	10	9	8	7	6	5	4	3	2	1

Contents

1

Postmodernism and the Need for Worldview Analysis

THE NATION THAT IS often hailed as the wealthiest, most powerful, and best-educated nation on earth is still one of the most religious—but in intriguing new ways. Nearly two-thirds of Americans say religion is very important in their lives, and close to half say they attend worship services at least once a week—the highest percentages since at least the 1960s. Other surveys indicate that belief in God and devotion to prayer are at historic highs. Further, voluntary giving to religious institutions—estimated to exceed $55 billion annually—surpasses the gross national product of many countries. From Los Angeles to New York City, there are more churches, synagogues, temples, and mosques per capita than in any other nation on earth (one for every 865 people).[1]

Additionally, more than four of every five Americans say they have "experienced God's presence or a spiritual force" close to them, and 46 percent say it has happened many times.[2] There appears to be a deep spiritual hunger in America. The modern world has failed many Americans who are reaching beyond themselves to find meaning and purpose in life.

But being religious today in America looks entirely different than it did only one hundred years ago when Protestantism, Catholicism, and Judaism dominated the religious landscape. America is now becoming the most religiously diverse nation on earth. Since the Immigration Act of 1965 eliminated quotas linked to national origin, Muslims, Buddhists, Hindus, Sikhs, Jains, Zoroastrians, and others have arrived in increasing numbers. Added to this reality is the fact that three in four Americans believe all religions have at least some elements of truth, even though few say they know much about any religions other than their own. Further, nearly 70 percent think spiritual experiences are the most important aspect of religion, not a written text or set of dogmas.[3]

With increased religious diversity has come increased emphasis on toleration. In a 2002 *US News & World Report*/PBS poll, 71 percent, including 70 percent of Christians, said Christians should be tolerant of people of other faiths and leave them alone. Only 22 percent (24 percent of them Christians) thought it was a Christian's duty to convert members of other faiths.[4] The point is that American culture, with its pluralistic nature and its diverse faiths, is changing—radically so.

A recent issue of *Time* magazine (October 13, 1997) focused on the growing appeal of Buddhism in America. In the words of one of its adherents, Buddhism is "a path of enlightenment into a lay culture without priests and temples and structures. . . . [It is a] daily practice of everyday life. . . . It's beneficial to all of us. It will go down in history as one of the best things that happened to civilization."[5] How can this be? Buddhism advocates the abandonment of logic and reason, glorifies emptiness and the illusion of selfhood, and looks toward the end of desire and liberation from rebirth. How could multitudes of Americans, including media gods like Steven Segal, Richard Gere, Tina Turner, and Phil Jackson, now embrace a system considered irrational not all that long ago? The answer is that America is now a postmodern, post-Christian civilization.

THE POSTMODERN WORLDVIEW

The whole Western world is in the midst of a paradigm shift from modernism to postmodernism. It is imperative that the church and its leaders understand this shift, for it impacts how we both relate to the culture in which we live and how we represent the Lord Jesus Christ in that culture. Postmodernism is not a generation of people; it is a way people view reality, a worldview. As a worldview it seeks to redefine truth and the place of the individual in the scheme of things.

Postmodernism is a reaction against modernism (or modernity). The modern period in Western history began with the Renaissance in northern Italy and northern Europe but exploded with the eighteenth-century Enlightenment. According to Millard Erickson[6] modernity abandoned the transcendent concept of reality, replaced supernaturalism with naturalism, championed humanism and individualism, and saw human knowledge as certain, objective, good, and attainable through the scientific method.

Theologian Stanley Grenz[7] poignantly sees modernism's human archetype in Mr. Spock, key hero in early versions of the popular TV series, *Star Trek*. The assumptions of the modern mind were that knowledge is certain and reasonable, objective and dispassionate, good and, therefore, optimistic. "Spock was the ideal Enlightenment man, completely rational and without emotions (or his emotions were in check). . . . According to the creators of *Star Trek*, in the end our problems are rational, and therefore, they require rational expertise." As with Spock, the Enlightenment saw human reason as the path to universal truth and universal morality. By contrast, postmodernism rejects the cold rationality of Mr. Spock and embraces a fuzzy tolerance of all truths.

Postmodernism as a worldview is complex and not easy to define; however, its ideas are pervasive and all-encompassing. What follows is an attempt to define the five specific characteristics of this emerging worldview now dominating Western civilization.

1. *A radical hermeneutic.* Rooted in the deconstructionist movement of post-World-War-II Europe, the postmodern hermeneutic (the science of interpretation; how humans interpret and understand the written word) sees words as power; words manipulate and control. This new hermeneutic argues that in communication, there is no final or true meaning to words. Therefore, the reader is sovereign. The reader determines the meaning of the text while the author's intent is nearly irrelevant. According to Alister McGrath,[8] "All interpretations are thus equally valid, or equally meaningless (depending on your point of view)."

For biblical Christianity, such a position is troublesome. Because authorial intent (i.e., God's verbal revelation in the Bible) is unknowable and irrelevant for the postmodernist, it is senseless to discuss the Bible as the Word of God. The postmodernist considers such a statement offensive and an attempt to control and manipulate. It is insensitive to those who see other sources of "truth," since in postmodernism, all claims to truth are equally valid; there is no universal vantage point for viewing truth. With this mind-set, a postmodernist will argue that it is arrogant and unacceptable for a Christian to claim the Bible as God's Word, as truth or as a source for truth. To accept the postmodern view of the written word is to destroy the foundation of genuine, biblical Christianity.

2. *A radical relativism.* Here is the focal point of postmodernism: the

doctrine of the autonomous self living in community. In postmodernism, the self defines reality. There are virtually no boundaries for behavior, and there are few authority figures that matter anymore. For example, the entire May 7, 2000, issue of *The New York Times Magazine* was devoted to this concept of autonomy. Autonomy impacts all aspects of culture—entertainment, business, law, leisure, and religion. I, the self, define all aspects of reality. There really is nothing transcendent that defines it for me; I am autonomous. This claim has a haunting ring of familiarity to it; in the book of Judges is the refrain, "Every man did what was right in his own eyes"(17:6; 21:25).

When individual autonomy is mixed with America's deep-seated commitment to rights and liberties, one sees how lethal this thinking becomes in the areas of sexuality, ethics, and morality. There are no boundaries or absolutes. Instead, the right of the individual is absolute. This belief frames discussion on the key cultural issues of our day—abortion, homosexuality, cohabitation before marriage, the use of genetic and reproductive technologies, and the right to "die with dignity." When "every man does what is right in his own eyes," the limits to freedom and rights are boundless.

A 2002 Zogby International poll of college seniors demonstrates the impact of this radical relativism. Nearly 73 percent of students surveyed said that when their professors taught ethics, the consistent message was that uniform standards of right and wrong do not exist.[9] Instead, what is right or wrong depends on differences in each individual and in the individual's culture. So, if all beliefs are equally valid, there is nothing to debate. Nothing separates personal "truth" from self-delusion. If students currently enrolled in college are convinced that ethical standards are simply a matter of individual choice, what hopes can we have that they will be reliably ethical in their future careers? This is the end result of a radical relativism.

3. *A radical pluralism.* The first two characteristics naturally lead to the third: a culture with a smorgasbord of religious choice where no worldview has a corner on truth. There are many "truths" and, since there is no certainty anyway, it does not matter which worldview you choose. Postmodernism stands for radical pluralism and universalism. In the postmodernist's mind, all religions are social constructs, and none is inherently superior to another. All religions are equally valid, and all paths lead to God. Religion, says the postmodernist, is not based on something external but stems from internal needs and subjective

personal experience. Religious people are therefore not discerning truth but rather are the source of their own truths, says the postmodernist. Something is true if it is true for me! ✓

Such a tenet explains why postmodern jargon is so pervasive in our culture. People often use terms with positive connotations—"diversity," "inclusion," and "multiculturalism"—to reinforce the claim that there is no truth and that no one can claim truth. Everyone's opinion is equally valid and worthy. Hence, increasingly Christians are bombarded with charges of being bigots and hatemongers because of the claim that Jesus is the way, the truth, and the life (John 14:6) and that Jesus is the only name under heaven by which men are saved (Acts 4:12). This is exclusive truth penetrating an inclusive world. It is exclusive truth, embodied in Jesus and proclaimed as such by His followers.

4. *A radical morality.* Postmodernism argues that moral and ethical behavior is not the result of any final reality such as God. Rather, morality comes from the needs of society. Every culture develops its own morals, and no other culture has the right to judge another's value system. True ethics are based on the needs of the moment, not final truth. ✓

Let me illustrate: Two recent articles in the *Chronicle of Higher Education* reveal that college students are often unwilling to oppose large moral horrors, including human sacrifice, ethnic cleansing, and slavery, because they believe no one has the right to criticize the moral views of another group or culture. Professor Robert Simon, who has taught philosophy for twenty years at Hamilton College in Clinton, New York, indicates that his students acknowledge that the Holocaust occurred but cannot bring themselves to say that killing millions of people is wrong. Between 10 and 20 percent deplore what the Nazis did, but their disapproval is expressed as a matter of taste or personal preference. One student responded, "Of course I dislike the Nazis, but who is to say they are morally wrong?" Another professor, Kay Haugaard of Pasadena College in California, wrote of a student in a recent literature class who said of human sacrifice, "I really don't know. If it was a religion of long standing. . . ." Haugaard was stunned that her student could not make a moral judgment: "This was a woman who wrote passionately of saving the whales, of concern for the rain forests, of her rescue and care for a stray dog."[10]

The result of postmodern pluralism and relativism is tolerance. You must respect the beliefs and distinctives of others. The only wrong belief is saying that someone else's beliefs are wrong. Postmodernism has replaced the ethic of truth with the ethic of tolerance. Toleration extends to lifestyle questions and practices. No wonder criticizing the homosexual lifestyle is labeled as bigoted and hate-filled. No wonder condemning abortion is labeled as threatening a woman's rights. No wonder challenging doctor-assisted suicide as dangerous is labeled naive.

But the Bible repudiates this type of thinking. It contains transcultural principles that form the ethical foundation for all civilizations. It is always wrong to murder, to lie, to commit adultery—no matter what culture one belongs to.

5. *A radical pragmatism*. Since there are no absolutes and every decision is based upon the needs of the moment, whatever works becomes "the new truth." The triumph of pragmatism therefore marks postmodernism. It does not matter if the United States president is immoral as long as he keeps the economy growing. If state-sponsored gambling causes destructive and addictive behavior, so be it; the profits are going to education and care for the elderly. Same-sex marriages are between consenting adults; if it works for them, fine. No one is being harmed by such practices.

Pragmatism is not a valid test for truth, for it can produce an end-justifies-the-means ethic. Following the tenets of postmodern pragmatism, the culture can justify the destruction of human embryos as a source for stem cells or gender selection of children in order to prevent hemophilia. Such practices will eventually empower parents to select their children as they select a car or a house. Give the specifications, and it is yours. God's revelation to the human race, recorded in the Bible, is the beginning point for truth's pursuit, not a pragmatic, end-justifies-the-means ethic.

THE NEED FOR WORLDVIEW ANALYSIS

The apostle Paul, in Colossians 2:8, issued a penetrating exhortation: "See to it that no one takes you captive through philosophy and empty deception, according to the tradition of men, according to the elementary principles of the world, rather than according to Christ." The relevance of this admonition is clear. We live in a world where "the tradition of men" and "empty deception" are pervasive. Wading through the current sea of worldly philosophies and traditions can be both perplexing and overwhelming—not to mention dangerous! How can a Christian keep from being deceived by worldviews that are opposed to the knowledge of Christ and His Word? How does one discern the differences between the competing worldviews of our postmodern age?

First, it is important to understand what a worldview actually is. A worldview is the core of what we believe. It answers the basic questions of life: How did we get here (creation and the universe)? Where are we going (the meaning of history)? What is the nature of reality (physical or spiritual or both)? What is the nature of God, or transcendent reality? What is the nature of truth (objective or subjective)? What is the nature of human beings? What happens to human beings when they die? What guidelines determine human behavior (ethics)? This book analyzes each of the major world religions, cults, and philosophical systems as a worldview. The history, major teachings, and ethical implications of each worldview will be considered. The ultimate thesis of this book is that only genuine biblical Christianity provides consistent answers to worldview questions. Only Christianity presents the truth.

Additionally, this book will suggest connection points, or bridges, for sharing the gospel within each worldview. The overall goal is to inform and equip Christians to live and witness the truth of the gospel in this postmodern world where all worldviews are tolerated.

BUILDING BRIDGES

Because Christianity proclaims exclusive truth, Christians must know how to build bridges to the postmodern world. Christians must understand this world and know how to make connections to it, while at the same time maintaining their distinctiveness as Christians. As Jesus counseled, we must "be in the world but not of the world" (see John 17:13-18).

The task of "building bridges" to the larger culture with its postmodern pluralism is very much a New Testament idea. Alister McGrath writes that the New Testament church is really a "colony of heaven. . . an outpost of heaven in a foreign land."[11] It speaks the language of that homeland and is governed by its laws. Yet, as Paul demonstrated in Acts 17:22-31, we are to seek common ground with citizens of earth, to be all things to all people that we might win some. For example, though the dangers of postmodernism are clear, this worldview is not all negative. Postmodernism allows an openness to supernatural realities and spiritual experiences that modernism would have scoffed at. The value postmodernists usually place on authentic relationships and community, an acceptance of diversity, personal experience, and practical living are not necessarily contrary to Christian values. The Christian must seize the opportunity and find this common ground with postmodernists.

Ultimately, we must speak and live the truth of the gospel in the world and into the worldviews of others. Using 1 Peter 3:15, Ken Boa[12] suggests a pattern for building bridges that will be helpful as you form relationships with those from different worldviews:

• "Sanctify Christ as Lord in your hearts." In other words, be certain Jesus is Lord of your life and affirm your utter dependence upon Him. Remember that when you are talking with someone embracing another worldview, this is a spiritual battle. Your task is to be faithful in proclaiming the truth. It is God's business to change the person.

• "Always be ready." Know God's Word and know how and when to use it. In doing so, you will be prepared to correct misconceptions about biblical Christianity.

• "To make a defense." Always keep the discussion focused on Jesus and His finished work on the cross. Stay away from minor issues and do your best to prevent the other person from focusing on his or her misconceptions. Stay focused in a friendly, God-honoring manner, and do not be sidetracked by the other person's unique claims or errors.

• "To every one who asks you." Pray that God will give you opportunities to share your faith in this pluralistic culture. Above all, be a good listener and ask for permission to express your view in the discussion. Do not be pushy or arrogant.

• "To give an account for the hope that is in you." It is your personal relationship with the living God that is the source of your power and strength. Do not be afraid to recount your personal experiences of all that God has done for you. He is your hope and strength.

• "Yet with gentleness and reverence." Show patience, respect, and love as you talk. Always look for common ground and seek to develop a relationship of trust and confidence that God can use to bring that person to Himself.

Never forget that Christians have the truth! Only genuine biblical Christianity provides consistent answers to worldview questions. This should give us confidence as we seek to gain understanding about different worldviews, build relationships, and make a stand for the truth in an age of many truths.

FOR FURTHER DISCUSSION

1. Summarize the cultural and ethnic changes that have occurred in America since the 1960s. What do you see as positives and negatives about these changes?
2. Cite real-life examples of each of the following five aspects of postmodernism from current news headlines, your own community, or past experiences.
   - Its radical hermeneutic
   - Its radical relativism
   - Its radical pluralism
   - Its radical morality
   - Its radical pragmatism
3. What is a worldview? Name some reasons why you think it is important to have a Christian worldview.
4. What are some "empty deceptions" the world gives as answers to the basic worldview questions?
5. In examining Ken Boa's pattern for building bridges, which points do you think would be the most challenging for you to practice? Why?

2

Naturalism
(or Secular Humanism)

IN HIS BOOK *Culture Wars*,[1] sociologist James Davison Hunter argues that American culture is experiencing a crisis of moral authority. One side of the cultural cleavage, "the progressive," claims that the individual self is the source of moral authority, while the other side, "the orthodox," claims that something transcendent is the source of moral authority. This struggle to define America's cultural center informs the debate over abortion, euthanasia, sexuality issues, education, law, and the role of government in our lives. It is a battle for the future.

The progressive side of this cleavage argues from a naturalistic perspective. There is an inherent antisupernaturalism in this position. For most people committed to modern thinking, physical matter is all there is. God does not exist, and religion is irrelevant. As religion fades, the progressive hopes, peace and harmony will reign. This sentiment is perhaps best captured in John Lennon's song "Imagine." In the lyrics, Lennon calls upon us to envision a time when there is "no heaven," "no hell," "no religion," and "nothing to kill or die for." What he calls the "brotherhood of man" will bring in an age of "no possessions," wealth, or greed; a time when the world "will be as one."

When did this worldview originate? What is its origin? One must go back to the Enlightenment of the eighteenth century for the answers.

THE EIGHTEENTH-CENTURY ENLIGHTENMENT: MODERN HUMANISM'S ORIGIN

The Enlightenment was a movement of ideas that saw its task as the release of humanity from error and prejudice, toward the achievement of truth, which in turn would produce freedom. Many Enlightenment thinkers targeted religion, for they believed it embodied the error and prejudice they loathed. They regarded Christianity and all other religions as irrational and inappropriate in a scientific age. The Enlightenment sought rational explanations for all of reality. They especially desired to examine human institutions to discover rational laws that governed society. Some of the principal thinkers of this age were Voltaire (1694-1778), Jean Jacques Rousseau (1712-1778), Denis Diderot (1713-1784), and David Hume (1711-1776).

Enlightenment thinkers were critical and skeptical of everything. Nothing in society escaped their analysis, including the church, the law, and the government. One French philosopher said, "all things must be examined, debated, investigated, without exception and without regard for anyone's feelings."[2]

Many of them also doubted the certainty of knowing absolute, universal truths that stemmed from religion. David Hume, the Scottish philosopher, epitomized this skeptical commitment by denying the rational certainty of experience, attacking arguments for God's existence, and authoring a blistering attack on a belief in miracles. Near the end of the Enlightenment, Immanuel Kant (1724-1804) also disputed traditional proofs for God's existence, claiming that one could not know God through reason, for there was no way to empirically verify His existence.

Finally, John Locke (1632-1704) embodied the devotion to empiricism, a decisive characteristic of the Enlightenment. For Locke, humans were born with no sense of right or wrong or any innate truths. Instead, the mind is like a blank slate that, through life, is filled with data coming from the senses. Following Locke, many Enlightenment thinkers repudiated all religion, including Christianity, as superstitious. It needed to be replaced with a rational system of ethics.[3]

THE INTELLECTUAL GODFATHERS OF HUMANISM

Three key historical figures have provided the underpinnings of this modern humanism that focuses strongly on the human mind to reason and solve problems. Each has solidified the modern conviction that religion, especially Christianity, has no place in a scientific age. Each has regarded religion as the enemy to progress and the higher achievements of the human race. Each has detested genuine biblical Christianity.

1. *The scientific attack.* Charles Darwin (1809-1882) undermined the authority of Scripture in the minds of many people, especially in

terms of its account of Creation. Before Darwin, most people in the Western world believed the design they observed in the physical world proved the existence of God and that everything had a fixed order or place. Each species was separately created by God, and each had a specific purpose in God's mind. Darwin's 1859 publication of *Origin of Species* shattered these assumptions. He argued that a struggle for existence characterized the natural world, resulting in organic beings adapting to the changing dynamics of their environment. Thus, by natural selection, unfavorable variations and those possessing them are eliminated. This process of natural selection over vast periods of time explains how different species evolve, he thought.

Darwin's theory of evolution had catastrophic effects for Christianity. First, it questioned the literal interpretations of the Bible, especially Genesis 1. Does "day" mean a twenty-four-hour day? Natural selection also argued against a special Creation of God as recorded in Genesis. As a result many doubted the Bible's authority. Second, natural selection sought to replace the idea of divine purpose and design in nature. Chance was offered as the powerful force controlling natural selection. Third, Darwin questioned the idea of order and fixity. For him nature was in a state of flux and change via natural selection; the word was *change*, not *permanence*. Fourth, Darwin's hypothesis was destructive to the idea of the uniqueness of man, so central to Christian theology. For Darwin, man was a product of time and chance. Key doctrines such as the image of God, the entrance of sin into the race through the Fall, and the need for a Savior were all questioned. Darwin shook Christianity at its foundation and made atheism respectable. Without Darwin, it is doubtful humanism would have been a viable option.[4]

2. *The political and economic attack.* Karl Marx (1818-1883), the founder of ideological communism, detested religion of all forms. He led one of the fiercest political and economic attacks on religion, specifically Christianity, in the modern world. He regarded religion as similar to opium; it drugged people. Because religion focused so much on heaven, it kept the working class down and, in Marx's view, was the excuse for their exploitation by the rich. For Marx, only the revolution energized by the working classes (the proletariat) would produce the perfect, communal society that he expected to emerge at the end of history. He believed the revolution would purge society of the evils of capitalism and produce the classless society that would bring history to its end.

3. *The psychological attack.* Sigmund Freud (1856-1939) led an unrelenting psychological attack on religion. An avowed atheist, Freud argued that religion was merely a psychological projection. Like a child runs to its father for protection in times of trouble, so humans project their earthly father into the heavens and run to him when things get tough. Freud believed that religious teaching had no basis in truth and that religion was really a sign of neurosis. Only his method of psychoanalysis, which probed beneath the subconscious, could help the person enslaved to religious dogma achieve the freedom Freud believed possible. His books, *The Future of an Illusion* and *Moses and Monotheism* provide his scathing attack on religious teachings.[5]

The scientific, political, economic, and psychological attack leveled by Darwin, Marx, and Freud have provided the intellectual basis for the ongoing revulsion most humanists have for religion, and especially for biblical Christianity. In some ways, the Christian church of North America is still reeling from these blistering attacks.

MODERN HUMANISM AS A WORLDVIEW: ITS THEOLOGY

What exactly does modern humanism or naturalism mean? At least historically, "a humanist" can be an "academic humanist" who studies the humanities—history, art, philosophy, or the classical languages. Such a scholar can be a Christian. Modern humanists should not be confused with "humanitarians," people who do good things for others. The humanists (naturalists) that this chapter addresses are those represented in the American Humanist Association, an organization created during the Enlightenment.

In 1933 a group of thirty-four liberal U.S. humanists drafted *The Humanist Manifesto I,* a document considered radical for its time. Committed to reason, science, and democracy, the document rejected orthodox religious dogma and argued for a "new statement of the means and purposes of religion."[6] This document was followed in 1973 by *The Humanist Manifesto II,* which not only reaffirmed the tenets of the 1933 document, but also raised the issues of civil liberties, equality, human survival, world economic growth, population and the environment, war and peace, and the building of a world community.

These two documents encapsulate the worldview of modernism. In short, modern humanism despises conventional religion and traditional morality. It rejects any belief in God and, instead, affirms a dogmatic and optimistic belief in humankind. Modern humanists see the problems of the world—racism, oppression, militarism, war, and poverty—as resolvable by humans working together for the maximum fulfillment of all. Traditional religion, whatever its form, they argue, has not made progress in solving these human problems. The modern humanist claims that we must put faith in ourselves and aggressively attack the problems of the human race. Such a spirit is evident in organizations such as the Americans for Democratic Action, the American Civil Liberties Union, and the National Organization for Women.

Despite the antisupernaturalism of modern humanism, this worldview still has a "theology." Here are its salient themes:

1. *Creation and the universe.* Humanists contend that the physical world was formed from chaos and that only man's reason has brought some order to this chaos. There is no divine plan or purpose. For the humanist, the only thing eternal is matter. Carl Sagan, who popularized the humanist approach to science and cosmic evolution, argued, "The Cosmos is all that is or ever will be."[7] Humanists say that all the matter of the universe has always existed in some form. In addition, this matter has no relationship to any transcendent creator.

The universe as we know it is a closed system, maintains Sagan.[8] It cannot be reordered from anything or anyone from outside itself. Of course, there is no transcendent God; humans are unable to reorder matter either. Sagan argues that because humans are matter and because there is no such thing as a soul (or anything supernatural), the laws of the universe apply to humans as well. Humans do not transcend the universe in any manner whatsoever. The universe is a closed system based on a uniform set of cause-effect relationships; humans are a part of that system.

2. *God.* Humanists insist that there is no personal God who created the universe or who gives any kind of meaning to it. They also reject the idea of God as sovereign, as one who organizes and oversees the course of history. As *The Humanist Manifesto II* asserts, "We find insufficient evidence for belief in the existence of the supernatural; it is either meaningless or irrelevant to the question of the survival and fulfillment of the human race. As nontheists, we begin with humans and not God, nature and not deity."[9] Thus, humans make their own history without any master plan. There is no accountability to God and no fear of judgment from Him.

3. *Humanity.* The human race is a cosmic accident, say the human-

ists. Humans come from nothing and, when they die, go to nothing. But that does not mean man is insignificant; indeed, humans are the key to a better world. Born with basic goodness, their intellects and attitudes only need to be positively shaped through their environment and education. *The Humanist Manifesto II* contends that "reason and intelligence are the most effective instruments that mankind possesses."[10] That is why modern humanism believes that compassion, cooperation, and community will bring about a better world. For that reason, economic well-being is possible in a world of "shared human values." There is no such thing as eternity; so modern humanism affirms that happiness is the only core value for the human race.

Humanism as a philosophy contends that "man is the measure of all things." In themselves, humans are the ultimate norm by which values are determined. They are the ultimate beings and the ultimate authority; all reality and all of life centers on human beings.

Curiously, although humans emerge from nothing and move toward nothing at death, somehow humans acquire supreme dignity. Yet, despite the humanist's belief in human progress, what is the real reason for hope? Why should we affirm human dignity? Why should I fight to solve the problems of racism, war, or poverty? If nothingness is my ultimate destiny, then human dignity is an illusion. Although emotionally satisfactory, humanism is intellectually dishonest and untenable.

4. *Ethics.* Modern humanism maintains that there are no absolutes to guide humans ethically. *The Humanist Manifesto II* demands that ". . . moral values derive their source from human experience. Ethics is *autonomous* and *situational,* needing no theological or ideological sanction. Ethics stem from human need and intent. To deny this distorts the whole basis of life. Human life has meaning because we create and develop our futures. . . . We strive for the good life, here and now."[11] For that reason, all human acts are ethically neutral, except for their influence on others for good or ill. But human standards are constantly changing, fluid, and vary from culture to culture. Hence, humans must create their own standards and then live consistently with them. Humanism rejects any dependence on absolute ethics; instead, sexual freedom, personal autonomy, and the unbridled pursuit of personal peace and happiness are the vital center of the humanist's ethical standard.

For decades humanism was the dominant worldview in most colleges and universities. It pervaded the discipline of science and underscored the humanities throughout Western civilization. It gives the impression of being objective, unbiased, and modern. Because modern scholarship has been so closely associated with humanism's tenets, to disagree with it is to appear backward and naive.

Today, however, in the typical college or university, postmodernism is competing with humanism. Where humanism has generally argued that truth is knowable, certain, and obtainable through the scientific method, postmodernism steps away from humanism's claim and argues that truth in any absolute or certain sense is not attainable. For that reason tolerance of all beliefs, worldviews, and systems is the reigning tenet of postmodernism. Both postmodernism and humanism seek human autonomy with no accountability. The relativism and pluralism of postmodernism mesh perfectly with the antisupernaturalism of humanism. The difference between the two is how each views the possibility of attaining absolute truth.

UNITARIANISM: HUMANISM AS AN ETHICAL SYSTEM

In many ways, the religious institutionalization of humanism (or naturalism) is the Unitarian worldview. The Unitarian worldview has its origins deep in early church history when many denied the triune nature of God. However, its modern form has its origin in late eighteenth- and early nineteenth-century New England. The theological descendants of the Puritans (the Congregationalists) denied the doctrine of the Trinity. The official movement was founded in 1825 as the American Unitarian Association, which merged with the Universalists in 1961. The movement acknowledges that it is no longer a part of the Christian worldview.

The Unitarian worldview has beliefs that make it the religious embodiment of naturalism (or humanism):

1. Unitarians deny that the Bible is God's Word. At best, it is a great piece of literature.

2. God is not triune. In fact, He is not a person. At best, Unitarians regard Him as a Force, or some Prime Mover. Unitarians often embrace atheism comfortably.

3. For the Unitarian, Jesus is a mere man. He is often thought of as a great teacher or ethicist but never as deity.

4. Unitarians argue that humans must look to themselves for their

"salvation," which means nothing more than the development of good character and living a good life. They reject the doctrine of hell and of God as a judge.

5. In short, Unitarians regard human reason as the sole authority for guidance and purpose in life. This worldview is naturalistic humanism dressed up as a religion with buildings, pastors, and teaching centered on the power of human reason.[12]

BUILDING BRIDGES TO HUMANISM

Bridge #1

Humanism affirms the value of human life and sees human happiness as its core value. This meshes with biblical Christianity, which also affirms the value of human life. However, humanism has no basis for its claim for the value of human life, for helping people, or for showing compassion. Why engage in such things if humans are simply the product of chance? Christianity affirms the value of life because humans bear God's image (Gen. 1:26ff). It provides the reason for compassion, care, and concern that is missing in humanism. Humanism is most vulnerable on this point and we must lovingly press it.

Bridge #2

Humanism claims that in terms of religious beliefs and ethical standards, it is impossible to have absolutes. In other words, there are absolutely no absolutes. In making such a claim, humanism affirms something absolute. That is a glaring inconsistency, and Christians can point this out. Christians can press humanists to seriously reflect on the inadequacy of a lack of standards for truth and ethics. Are humanists willing to bank everything on the belief that there is no God? What if there is? What if there is accountability? The Holy Spirit can use this inconsistency within humanism to bring conviction.

Bridge #3

Humanism teaches that at death there is extinction. The only "immortality" for the human, says *The Humanist Manifesto II,* is to "continue to exist in our progeny and in the way our lives have influenced others in our culture."[13] There is no hope of seeing loved ones, of life after death, or of an eternal destiny. Humanism provides no real incentives for living or for dying. This physical world is all there is, they argue, and we must live for the moment. If there is no God, then there is no account-ability and no motivation for virtue or goodness. Most people cannot live with this kind of teaching.

Here Christianity's message is compelling. It offers hope because there is life after death; there is hope of seeing loved ones and friends. Christianity also offers the certainty of salvation, which guarantees heaven, eternal life with God. Humanism offers no counsel to a family who has lost an infant in death, to someone with a terminal illness, or to a wife who has lost her husband in an automobile accident. The humanist can offer nothing; Christianity offers everything. It is in the real world that humanism's bankruptcy becomes evident.

Naturalism (or humanism) pervades Western civilization and is still currently institutionalized in many of the academic centers. It remains powerful, influential, and informs much of contemporary edu-cation. It will retain its position of importance only as long as Westerners seek their purpose and meaning from technology, science, and reason. Its antisupernaturalism is difficult for most people, how-ever, because the average person cannot live without some sense of a transcendent realm, belief that there is something beyond death, that the physical is not all there is. Only genuine biblical Christianity answers that quest for meaning and purpose.

FOR FURTHER DISCUSSION

1. What were some of the goals and characteristics of the eighteenth-century Enlightenment?
2. Why was it difficult for the Enlightenment person to embrace reli-gion, especially biblical Christianity? What evidence do you see of this same tendency in people you know today?
3. Crystallize the essence of *The Humanist Manifesto I* and *The Humanist Manifesto II* into one or two sentences. What would you say as a pos-sible rebuttal to these documents?
4. How is the humanist's view of humanity similar to and different from the Christian view? Use Scripture to support your observations.
5. Which humanist views or humanist figures (Freud, Marx, Darwin, etc.) do you see as most influential today?
6. What bridge (from the book or your own ideas) might you use to build a connection with a Unitarian friend?

3

Hinduism

HINDUISM IS PERHAPS the most complex and difficult worldview to understand, especially to the Western, rational mind. It seems to hold frequently contradictory tenets and is the most difficult to summarize in a short book. Hinduism gradually grew over a period of five thousand years, absorbing and assimilating the religious and cultural movements of India. It has been likened to "a vast sponge, which absorbs all that enters it without ceasing to be itself. . . . Like a sponge it has no very clear outline on its borders and no apparent core at its center."[1]

In order to understand the basic tenets of Hinduism, we need an outline of the main Hindu scriptures and its history. After this brief review of Hinduism's history, we will review its theology and its ethical implications.

HINDUISM: ITS SCRIPTURES AND ITS HISTORY

Scriptures

The Hindu scriptures, mainly written in Sanskrit, were composed over a period of more than 2,000 years. The name for the most sacred scriptures of Hinduism is the "Vedas," meaning "book of knowledge." There are four Vedas: the Rig-Veda, the Sama-Veda, the Yajur-Veda, and the Atharva-Veda. These sacred texts written before 1000 B.C. contain the life, customs, and beliefs of early polytheists who inhabited ancient India. They also contain the liturgies, chants, prayers, and litanies associated with the worship of their many gods. Hindus usually regard the Veda texts as verbally and unerringly authoritative.

From 1000 to 800 B.C. another group of holy texts emerged called the Brahmanas. The focus of these texts is the sacrifices that Hindus must perform. The Brahman priests were given the authority and responsibility to perform animal sacrifices to the gods to appease them and ensure salvation.

Mature philosophical Hinduism emerged with the writing of the best-known Hindu texts—the Upanishads—written between 800 and 600 B.C. These texts have little regard for the ritual, formal religion of the earlier holy books; instead, they are philosophical writings that emphasize an understanding of the world and the realm of the transcendent. With the Upanishads, the important Hindu term "Brahman" came to designate the one Reality or World-Soul. Brahman (sometimes identified as "Atman") is the absolute, infinite, eternal, omnipresent, impersonal, indescribable, neuter Being of the universe. Individual human souls, the Upanishads teach, are to merge with Atman to achieve salvation (more about this later).

About 250 B.C., the Code of Manu emerged as a sacred text. The Code gives the commandments and prohibitions that regulate the daily living of the Hindu through all of life's stages. Social regulations, dietary rules, and interpersonal rules of behavior reinforced the emerging caste system within ancient India. Indeed, the four-fold caste system is presented in the Code with great elaboration and approval.

Among the many sacred Hindu texts, the Bhagavad-Gita is perhaps the most revered. It is part of the epic devotional literature that emerged around the time of Christianity's origin. The Gita records the ongoing discussion between the Hindu hero-warrior-god Krishna and Arjuna, his kinsman, friend, and disciple. The dialogue reinforces a commitment to India's historic caste system and reincarnation, and can be summarized as "Do your caste duty, and trust your God for the rest of your salvation." With the Gita, Hinduism had become devotional and duty-oriented.[2]

History

Ancient Hinduism (2000-500 B.C.). In this period we see the worship of half-personified forces of nature such as fire, wind, and rain, and a primitive conception of the Absolute, the One. All things were a part of this impersonal One. Another important development of this period is the conception of a cosmic order of which the Hindu gods were the guardians. A professional class of priests became necessary to propitiate these gods with sacrifices.

During this time the Upanishads were written, which turned the Hindu searchlight inward. Hindus discovered that at the center of their being, beyond the senses, beyond the mind, and beyond understanding is a divine spirit. The goal of Hinduism is to liberate the human divine spirit—the true end of man. At the end of this period in history, the gods and sacrifices faded into the background. What emerged was the focus on self, the law of karma, and the commitment to reincarnation.

The Sutra and Epic Period (500 B.C. to A.D. 300). During this period the epics of Hinduism, especially the Bhagavad-Gita, promoted a great religious revival throughout India as the stories, legends, and teachings of the Upanishads became popular and understandable among the people. Also during this period, the multiple gods and goddesses from the various parts of India became incorporated into the Hindu pantheon of gods. The use of images, temples, pilgrimages to sacred places associated with deities, and festivals took hold in Hindu India. Thus the main tangible features of Hinduism found in modern India came into being.

Medieval Hinduism (A.D. 300 to 1400). During this long period, Hinduism faced three enemies—Buddhism, Jainism, and Islam. Although still found in India today, Buddhism and Jainism, both of which emerged from within Hinduism, were defeated as challenges to Hindu supremacy. But that was not the case with Islam.

Islam raced throughout India from A.D. 1000 through 1400, causing a period of turmoil in the course of Hindu history. Hindus suffered terribly from Islamic fanaticism. There were forced conversions, destruction of temples, and the desecration of holy places. Major parts of Hindu India were lost to Islam.

Modern Hinduism (A.D. 1400 to the present). The British takeover of India, which lasted about a century and a half, was quite unlike the Muslim conquest. The British broke the isolation of India and brought Hinduism into contact with European history, science, and literature, and exposed it to European political and social institutions, customs, and manners. The British rule profoundly changed India and Hinduism.

During this period, the caste system was severely criticized, as were practices such as the burning of widows on the funeral pyres of their husbands. Also, during the modern period, Hindu ideas and thoughts began to influence Western thinking as well. We see that influence in Ralph Waldo Emerson and the Transcendental movement of nineteenth-century New England.

Finally, Mahatma Gandhi changed India and Hinduism. Gandhi, in leading the fight for independence from Britain, extended the virtue of nonviolence to communities and nations and developed a suitable technique of action for it. According to Gandhi, truth is God, and non-violence is the means of reaching it. Perfect nonviolence is perfect self-realization. His nonviolent methods produced the democratic India that still exists today.[3]

HINDUISM AS A WORLDVIEW: ITS THEOLOGY AND ETHICS

Hindu theology is complex and difficult for the Western mind. Foundational to Hinduism is the concept of Brahman. Brahman is the unchanging reality of the universe. It is the unity that is in the universe and yet beyond it. All objects, animate and inanimate, are included in it. Gods, humans, demons, animals, etc. are all part of Brahman. (The term "Brahman" derives from a language root that means "to expand," denoting an entity that cannot be limited in magnitude or expansion.)

In the Upanishads, Brahman is represented in two aspects—in an unqualified state named *Nirguna* Brahman, and in a qualified sense named *Saguna* Brahman. Nirguna Brahman is indescribable in human terms. Nirguna is attributeless. It is described by negation (i.e., by that which it is not—no body, no form, no attributes). It is beyond space, time, and causation; it is infinite and unknowable. The Upanishads describe Nirguna as:

> Where one sees nothing else, hears nothing else, understands nothing else—that is the Infinite.
> Where one sees something else, hears something else, that is the finite.[4]

Central to Hinduism's understanding of Brahman is that Nirguna Brahman is veiled; that is, its "maya" (veil) hides the true nature of Brahman and causes the perception in humanity that the physical world is true reality, when in fact Nirguna Brahman, the realm of the true Infinite, is reality. Thus, Saguna Brahman is the veiled Brahman.

Because of Saguna Brahman, Hindus can speak of creation and its various deities. Saguna Brahman is the personal "god" who watches over the physical universe and acts as its ruler. When one speaks of attributes of deity, one is speaking of Saguna Brahman. For that reason, as well, Saguna Brahman is familiarly known as Brahma the Creator, Vishnu the Preserver, and Shiva the Destroyer. All three of these "gods" are simply different ways of looking at Saguna, the veiled Brahman.

The "Avataras" are the incarnations of the gods. The Avataras are crucial especially to understanding Vishnu. One of his most popular Avataras is Krishna, the hero of the epic Bhagavad-Gita. The following chart attempts to visualize the difficult theology of Hinduism.[5]

NIRGUNA BRAHMAN
(Impersonal Brahman)

THE VEIL OR "MAYA"

SAGUNA BRAHMAN
(Personal Brahman with attributes)

BRAHMA   VISHNU   SHIVA

For the Western, rational mind, one major question looms in Hinduism: How can there be beliefs in different gods (Hindu polytheism) along with the belief in oneness so central to the Hindu idea of Nirguna Brahman? Malcolm Pitt argues that

> Because of the relative unreality of God himself in the theistic sense, the realization that all concepts of God are human and all creatures are Brahman, it seems to be only natural that the Hindu can tolerate the worship of any form of any kind as a manifestation of Reality. This is the framework that allows the most advanced Indian philosopher to feel that the most primitive animist, in living up to his best light, is *on the path* to the realization of Reality.[6]

Although Hinduism seems polytheistic, in reality its theology contends that there is one monistic Nirguna Brahman. Ultimately all religions and all beliefs reflect some kind of "path" to that Reality. Hence the "sponge" we know as Hinduism.

What follows are some cardinal definitions essential to understanding Hinduism:

• "God"—In Hinduism the Supreme Being is the Impersonal Nirguna Brahman, a philosophical Absolute beyond all impediments, either ethical or metaphysical.

• "Humanity"—The human is an emanation or temporary manifestation of the Impersonal Brahman. Humans are not inherently or permanently valuable; nor is the human accountable to "god."

• "The World"—The physical world is a temporary, worthless illusion due to the veil (or "maya") that hides the Impersonal Brahman.

• "Reincarnation" or "samsara" is the belief in the transmigration of the soul. There is a cycle of rebirth after rebirth after rebirth of the soul. One could be reborn as a wealthy aristocrat or as an animal, a beetle, worm, vegetable, etc.

• "Karma" is the cause of what is happening in one's life now. The Law of Karma (*karma* means "works, deeds") is the law that one's thoughts, words, and deeds have an ethical consequence fixing one's lot in future existences. Karma is what determines the nature of the next birth in the cycle. The Law of Karma is at the heart of the Hindu ethical system.

• "Moksha" is the release from the cycle of reincarnation, the cycle of life. It is salvation from illusion and release into the true reality of Nirguna Brahman.

• "Nirvana" is not a place but a state in which self-awareness is lost and oneness with Brahman attained.

• The "caste system" originated around 500 B.C. and constituted the fundamental social system of Hindu India. There were four main castes and a group called the "outcastes," or the "untouchables," obviously outside the four main castes. As Hinduism developed, the Law of Karma was tied to the caste system. Today the caste system is technically illegal in India, but its manifestations linger in the Indian social order.[7]

INROADS FROM THE EAST

Many Hindu concepts and practices have penetrated the Western world. In some ways, Hinduism has mainstreamed into Western thinking. Here are several examples:

Yoga. Yoga is not unique to Hinduism but is a fundamental technique for achieving Hindu spirituality. Norman Anderson describes yoga as "the physiological and psychological technique by which all bodily and psychic energy is controlled in order to achieve spiritual perfection."[8] Ultimately spiritual perfection is reunion with Brahman. Through the control of body and mind, the human can achieve a state of being that transcends space and time. The soul is thereby freed from attachment to the physical world of illusion. In the purest form of yoga, all mental activity stops, and the mind is completely still.

As a means of relaxation, to relieve stress, or even prescribed medically for muscle relaxation, yoga is popular in the West today. Christians must be careful and discerning about practicing yoga.

Reincarnation. Reincarnation tied with the Law of Karma has also been popularized in the West. It is manifested in three ways: (1) For some, karmic reincarnation provides an explanation for birth defects, physical handicaps, poverty, social injustice, and suffering. (2) Many today argue that humans "remember" their past lives in previous reincarnations. Feelings of *deja vu,* or a strong sense that one has been somewhere before, are additional proofs for reincarnation, some argue. (3) Some even argue that the Bible teaches reincarnation. John the Baptist and Melchizedek are viewed as reincarnations of Elijah and Jesus. The doctrine of being "born again" in John 3 is pointed out as evidence of Christianity accommodating Hindu reincarnation. The late Edward Cayce popularized such teachings in his books and lectures.[9]

Transcendental Meditation (TM). TM is the brainchild of Maharishi Mahesh Yogi, who was born in North Central India in 1917 and forty years later traveled to Europe and America preaching his gospel of TM. Different from yoga, TM practitioners use a "mantra," a secret Sanskrit word that is repeated over and over silently in the mind to achieve expanded consciousness. TM is often portrayed as a nonreligious exercise to relieve stress and to relax. TM promises greater clarity of perception, expanded awareness, and full development of the individual. The goal is natural bliss and happiness.

TM is presented as being nonreligious, but that is far from the truth. To Maharishi, humans are innately good, and TM enables one to reach that state of goodness through meditation using the mantra. Such teaching clearly contradicts the biblical teachings on sin, salvation, and the nature of humanity.

BUILDING BRIDGES TO HINDUS

The Christian gospel is clear and straightforward, but it is the convincing and convicting work of the Holy Spirit that brings a person to Christ. As we share Christ in both word and deed, it is imperative to remember that our prayers and our dependence on the Spirit bear the fruit of the gospel. Nonetheless, there are critical bridges or contact points of similarity between Christianity and Hinduism that the Spirit can use:

Bridge #1

As with Christians, Hindus believe that ultimate reality is spirit. John 4:24 teaches that "God is spirit and those who worship Him must worship in spirit and truth." That there is a spiritual world and that that world is ultimate reality is a powerful commonality between the two faiths.

Bridge #2

Central to Hinduism is the idea of a unity to all things, a unity centered in the belief in Nirguna Brahman. Given this conviction, the Christian can build the bridge that natural revelation reveals this unity, focused on God Himself (see Psalm 19 and Romans 1:18ff.). The next critical step is, of course, to get the Hindu to focus on the special revelation in Jesus Christ.

Bridge #3

Rooted in the Law of Karma, Hinduism also teaches that there is a sense of justice that permeates the universe. If the Hindu falls short of karma's requirements, he or she is condemned to the endless cycle of reincarnation. For the Christian, that sense of justice has been met in the finished work of Jesus Christ on Calvary's cross.

Bridge #4

Seeking to break the cycle of the soul's transmigration, Hinduism has a passion for freedom. For Christianity, Jesus provides that longing for freedom. Faith in Jesus Christ provides the freedom from sin and its bondage (see John 8:32).

Bridge #5

Hinduism teaches and respects the significant cost there is to the religious life. The typical Hindu honors and defers to the devout, the holy, and the ascetic leaders of the Hindu faith, for they are close to breaking the Law of Karma and achieving the freedom from reincarnation. Although Christianity rejects the extreme asceticism of Hinduism, it does teach "death to self," other-centeredness, and self-sacrificial love as paramount virtues. Hindus can identify with these teachings and witness the liberation from legalism that biblical Christianity brings.

These five bridges are most helpful in sharing Christianity with Hindus, but there are three significant barriers to which Christians must be sensitive. Only God's Spirit can break down these barriers, but Christians must be conscious of them and their power.

1. Most Hindus believe that ultimate truth is a synthesis of many truths. They separate the Jesus revealed in history from the Christ of the Christian faith. To them, Jesus is not the only path to truth or to salvation. Christians reject this syncretism, believing God's revelation is the only source for truth.

2. Many Hindus believe that all religions lead to the same goals and that none possess full truth. Often Hindus contend that Jesus is *a* way to salvation but will not tolerate the claim that He is *the* way of salvation. This is perhaps the most formidable barrier between Christianity and Hinduism. For Christians Jesus is exclusive, and His path of salvation is exclusive (John 14:6).

3. Hindus believe that there is divine revelation in all religions and that none can claim exclusivity. Therefore, Christianity is not unique. But, because it is rooted in revelation, Christianity is unique and exclusive. With love and compassion, this truth must be shared. Only God's Spirit can break down this barrier.[10]

As stated at the beginning of this chapter, Hinduism resembles a sponge, soaking up teachings, absorbing them, and then redefining them according to its syncretistic teachings. If Christians are to reach Hindus, we must understand their thinking, build the bridges, and then allow the Holy Spirit to do His supernatural work. There is no other way to reach the Hindu for Jesus Christ.

FOR FURTHER DISCUSSION

1. What does the author mean when he compares Hinduism to a sponge?
2. Compare and contrast the sacred texts of Hinduism with the Christian Scriptures.
3. Which period of Hinduism's history was most interesting to you? Why?
4. Describe three of the following terms according to Hindu theology. Compare and contrast these terms with Christian theology.
   - God
   - humans
   - the world

- reincarnation
- Moksha
- The Law of Karma

5. Which of the three "inroads from the East" do you think has had the most influence on Western culture? Give an example of this influence.

6. Keeping in mind some of the bridges and barriers to Hinduism cited in this chapter, write a paragraph on how you would share your faith with a Hindu. Spend time in prayer for opportunities to witness to Hindus.

4

Buddhism

FOR THE TYPICAL WESTERNER, Buddhism is the faint memory of people prostrated before a large statue of a smiling man sitting cross-legged or of men in yellow robes with their hands together, meditating. Yet 300 million people call themselves Buddhists in Asia, and the numbers are increasing in the Western world. It is a religion that predates Christianity by almost six centuries. What is this curious faith called Buddhism? Why do so many Westerners find it appealing? How should we as Christians seek to reach the Buddhist with the gospel of Christ?

Richard Gard defines Buddhism as follows:

> Conceived in Asia, Buddhism is an historic expression of a universal human ideal. It offers any individual or society a voluntary way of thought and conduct, based upon an analysis of conditioned existence, dependent upon supreme human effort, and directed toward the realization of freedom in perfect existence.[1]

From its beginnings, Buddhism differed from most other religions. Rather than focusing on moral evil, it concentrated on pain and suffering; unlike other religions, Buddhism did not ask for devotion to or ritual toward a supreme god or gods. Buddhism is essentially a philosophy rather than a religion, an Eastern form of spirituality. David Bentley Taylor characterizes Buddhism as "a non-theistic ethical discipline, a system of self-training . . . stressing ethics and mind-culture to the exclusion of theology."[2]

BUDDHISM: ITS HISTORY

Buddhism was born in the sixth century B.C., one of the most significant centuries in human history. Babylon had collapsed as a world power in 538 B.C. only to be replaced by two Eastern powers—India and China.

In this century, India moved from tribal oligarchies to a monarchy and an empire. Within India at this time a monetary system, trade and commerce, and a class of merchants and royal advisors emerged. Hinduism was being challenged, and a new, reflective, and meditative form of Hinduism was emerging, illustrated especially by the Upanishads (see chapter 3).

In addition, within Hinduism a movement of celibate asceticism developed. These new ascetics lived by begging and did not worship any deities. They maintained that the ascetic lifestyle of self-denial brought about liberation from reincarnation. According to Richard Robinson and Willard Johnson, these ascetic Hindus "believed in transmigration [i.e., reincarnation] and maintained that life is misery and liberation from the cycle of birth and death is supreme good."[3]

Into this historical context Siddhartha Gautama, the founder of Buddhism, was born in northern India. Although disputed, his probable dates are 566 to 486 B.C. Early Buddhist thought and history were transmitted through oral tradition and not written down until later. So the life of Siddhartha contains extensive legends mixed with historical fact. Apparently born into a wealthy family, Siddhartha lived in comfort through his youth, until he was confronted with a crisis. When challenged with "the four most impressive sights"—a man advanced in age, a sick man, a dead body, and an ascetic hermit—he abandoned his comfort, his wife, and child to seek life's meaning, specifically to answer the questions of suffering and death.[4]

Siddhartha sought answers in Hinduism. He shaved his head, put on a yellow robe, and tried asceticism for five years. John Noss describes some of his devotional acts during this period:

> He lived for periods on all sorts of nauseous foods, dressed in chafing and irritating garments, stood for days in one posture . . . sat on a couch of thorns, lay in the cemetery on charred bones among rotting bodies, let dirt and filth accumulate on his body till it dropped off of itself, and even ate his own excrement in the extremity of self-discipline.[5]

However, after five years, he realized the futility of asceticism and abandoned the effort. According to legend, Siddhartha's awakening came while he was sitting under a Nigrodha tree (or Bo tree). There he won his battle with desire and attained the knowledge of perfect contentment, becoming a *Buddha*, which means "enlightened one." He had discovered a "middle path" between those who taught sensuality (indulging oneself) and those who taught asceticism (denying oneself). His Buddhist monastic order (i.e., the order of the enlightened ones) had begun. It spread quickly throughout India, and Buddha spent the rest of his life preaching the "middle path." He died at the age of eighty.

Siddhartha Buddha was profoundly concerned with explaining suffering—its cause and how to escape it.[6] His answer was the Four Noble Truths:

1. Suffering is universal. The act of living is suffering, and each person's incarnation is suffering. Therefore, "salvation" (Nirvana) is release from this cycle of suffering.

2. The cause of suffering is craving (selfish desire). The endless cycle of reincarnation is tied to this desire, this craving, because humans are attached to this world.

3. The cure for suffering is to eliminate craving. Buddha's great discovery was that to live is to suffer, and craving causes suffering; therefore, remove craving, and suffering will cease.

4. Eliminate craving by following the Middle Path—the Noble Eightfold Path. This Eightfold Path consists of three categories: understanding, morals, and concentration:

- *Understanding:* right viewpoint, right aspiration
- *Morals:* right speech, right behavior, right occupation, right effort
- *Concentration:* right-mindedness, right meditation.

Buddha taught that those who followed this Eightfold Path would eventually attain Nirvana, the release from the endless cycle of birth and death.[7]

Buddha's teaching about the Four Noble Truths and the Eightfold Path was extremely general, readymade to fit with other moral codes of behavior. Buddha spent his life trying to explain them. According to John Noss, Buddha's rules were simple. All followers were to wear a yellow robe, shave their heads, carry a begging bowl, take part in daily meditation, and subscribe to the Buddhist confession: "I take refuge in the Buddha; I take refuge in the Dharma (the Law); I take refuge in the Order." Buddhists were also to obey the Ten Precepts: Refrain from destroying life, don't take what is not given, be chaste, be honest, do not drink intoxicants, do not eat after noon, do not watch dancing or singing or drama, do not wear ornaments or scents or garlands, do not have a high or broad bed, and do not possess any silver or gold.[8]

Buddhism spread rapidly throughout Asia. Siddhartha strongly opposed India's caste system, so closely tied to Hinduism. He taught that Nirvana was for everyone, regardless of caste. Hence Buddhism appealed to the lower castes of society. In addition, unlike the vague, often contradictory ideas of Hinduism, Buddhism offered a precise definition of the human condition with an exact plan of "salvation." Finally, Buddhist monks took their new religion along the trade routes of China, Japan, and Tibet. Today more than 300 million Buddhists live in the areas from Sri Lanka to Japan because of these traveling monks.[9]

Buddhism is divided into two major sects, with many other variations. Those two sects are Hinayana Buddhism and Mahayana Buddhism:

• Hinayana (Theravada) Buddhism means "the doctrine of the lesser way," suggesting that only a fortunate few will find Nirvana—those who commit wholeheartedly to Buddha's teachings. This sect (sometimes called Theravada Buddhism) stresses the monastic life and has become wealthy through gifts of land and money for the monasteries. It is dominant today in Sri Lanka, Myanmar, Thailand, Cambodia, and Laos.

• Mahayana Buddhism means the teaching of the "greater way." Its followers know that Buddha taught that salvation is for all people, but they believe that Buddha himself was special. In fact, in this branch of Buddhism, Buddha is deified. They argue that Buddha remained on earth for forty-five years after his enlightenment despite the fact that he could have gone on to Nirvana. He chose to save humans. Therefore, Buddha is not only a teacher (as he is in Hinayana), but he is a savior-god for all people. He is still accessible through prayer and worship and continues to impart insight and revelation to his followers. This sect of Buddhism is far more popular and influential. Today it is dominant in China, Tibet, Japan, Vietnam, and Korea.[10]

BUDDHISM AS A WORLDVIEW: ITS THEOLOGY

God: Despite the manifold divisions within Buddhism, there is a basic metaphysical worldview underlying the entire Buddhist framework. Although in many ways Buddhism is nontheistic (as evidenced by no definable belief in a supreme being or god), it promotes pantheism. Pantheism is the belief that God (ultimate reality) is the world, and the world is ultimate reality (i.e., God); God is all and all is God. However, within Buddhism any religious devotion or piety is not directed to this pantheistic "god." There are no prayers or sacrifices to deities in Buddha's teachings. For Buddha, the universe abounded in gods, goddesses, demons, and other nonhuman powers and agencies, but all were without exception finite and subject to death and rebirth.[11] So Buddhism is foundationally pantheistic but practically nontheistic.

Salvation: For the Buddhist, salvation centers on the individual, on his or her own powers, on redemption through spiritual self-discipline. Buddha was not interested in philosophical speculations regarding salvation. He was immensely interested in the practical and the psychological dimensions of life, namely suffering and how to escape it. Although he rejected Hinduism and all it represented, Buddha did adopt (with alterations) two prominent religious thoughts from Hinduism— the Law of Karma and rebirth.

Concerning the Law of Karma (the law of cause and effect), Buddha viewed it as operating remorselessly and without recompense in the life of unchecked desire. The desires and lusts that caused so much suffering would act in determining the next cycle's destiny for the human. But if the person got control of his desires through the Middle Path that Buddha taught, the cycle of rebirth could be broken.

It is clear that Buddha believed in the doctrine of reincarnation. However, in his teachings, he refused to discuss exactly what happened to the self—the true essence of the person—at death and at the next cycle of reincarnation. For the Western rational mind, there is simply no analogy or satisfactory explanation for Buddha's reincarnation teaching. John Noss offers a helpful perspective:

> Wherever we observe it, the living world, whether about us or within ourselves, is constantly in flux, in a state of endless becoming. There is no central planning world-self, no sovereign Person in the heavens holding all together in unity. There is only the ultimate impersonal unity of Being itself, whose peace enfolds the individual self when it ceases to call itself "I" and enters the featureless purity of Nirvana, as a drop of spray is merged in its mother sea.[12]

For Buddhists, "salvation" is this "drop of spray merging in its mother sea." "Salvation" is the breaking of the reincarnation cycle, the liberation from pain and suffering, the merging with "the ultimate impersonal unity of Being," and the attainment of Nirvana. Nirvana to the Buddhist is a state of perfect, painless peace and joy, a self-achieved freedom from misery of any kind. Nirvana is an eternal state of neither being nor nonbeing; it is the end of all finite states. As Noss argues,

"Human knowledge and human speech could not compass it."[13] Nirvana divests self of self in any sense of the word.

Scripture: The Buddhist idea of scripture and revelation do not correspond to most other faiths, including Christianity. Buddhist teacher, Subhadra Bhikshu, writes:

> No; there are no divine revelations. It is a groundless assumption, utterly rejected by Buddhism, that the truth should be revealed by God or an angel, to a few inspired favorites. The only revelation we have ever received is from the mouth of those sublime teachers of mankind, who themselves have worked out their own perfection and deliverance, having shown others the way to do it. . . .[14]

Subhadra Bhikshu summarizes Buddhism's theology:

> Buddhism teaches the reign of perfect goodness and wisdom without a personal God, continuance of individuality without an immortal soul, eternal happiness without a local heaven, the way of salvation without a vicarious Savior, redemption worked out by each one himself without any prayers, sacrifices, and penances, without the ministry of ordained priests, without the intercession of saints, without Divine mercy. Finally, it teaches that supreme perfection is attainable even in this life and on this earth.[15]

BUDDHISM: ITS ETHICS

Fundamentally, Buddhism is about ethics. It is a religion founded on human ethical behavior as the sole basis for attaining Nirvana. If one were to put it in Christian terms, Buddhism is a works-righteousness system of salvation. Nirvana (salvation) is totally dependent on what the Buddhist achieves while pursuing the Middle Path of Buddha's teaching. A person who follows the Four Noble Truths and the Eightfold Path will attain Nirvana. If a person remains captive to human desires, the Law of Karma will remain active, resulting in ongoing reincarnation.

By maintaining a commitment to the Four Noble Truths and observing the Eightfold Path, Buddhists naturally follow Buddha's Ten Precepts (discussed previously). Buddhists live between self-indulgence on the one hand (which is condemned) and extreme practices of ascetic self-denial (which are equally condemned). Buddha claims that this balance produces the psychological freedom within this life and the hope of release from reincarnation that awaits the faithful. More than any other religion, except perhaps Confucianism, Buddhism is a religion of ethics, a religion of what the faithful *ought* to do.

BUILDING BRIDGES TO BUDDHISTS

The ultimate reason for seeking an intelligent understanding of Buddhism, or any worldview, is to find bridges we can build to reach people with the gospel. Jesus did this constantly as He regularly adapted His message to His hearers.

Bridge #1

First and foremost, Christians must set consistent examples. What we believe—our convictions—must be demonstrated in a Christlike life. Because Buddhism is fundamentally an ethical faith with no real emphasis on the supernatural, the authentic life of Christ speaks volumes to followers of Buddha. Authenticity will get the Buddhist's attention.

Bridge #2

Both Buddhism and Christianity address the issue of suffering. For the Buddhist, suffering encompasses all of life from birth to death. Clinging to the pleasures of life is considered foolishness and vain. The Christian worldview shows some harmony with Buddhism on this point. Christianity recognizes the reality of suffering and ties it to the consequences of human sin (Gen. 3). For that reason the book of Ecclesiastes may be the best starting point, for it declares the futility of life "under the sun" (1:1-11). The author of Ecclesiastes points out that life is unfair, futile, confusing, and transitory. It is only belief in a sovereign, personal God that brings sense to all of this. For that reason, life is seen, for the Christian, as a good gift from a good God who ultimately makes sense even out of suffering. Perhaps books like Philip Yancey's *Where Is God When It Hurts?* or C. S. Lewis's *The Problem of Pain*, both of which deal with suffering, can be of help to the Buddhist.

Bridge #3

When the Buddhist asks the question, "What is life all about?" he looks inside himself for the answers. When the Christian asks the same question, he turns to God for the answer. Buddhists focus on dwelling on and mastering self in an effort to eradicate self. The haunting question for the Buddhist is: How does one achieve selflessness through occupation with self? It is a paradox.

Jesus solves the paradox: "He who has found his life shall lose it and he who has lost his life for my sake shall find it" (Matt. 10:39; Mark 8:35; Luke 9:24). We find our true identity by losing ourselves in the One who created us, namely Jesus Christ.

Bridge #4

Buddhism claims that all humans should be treated well. But why? There is no absolute standard in Buddhism. By paying respect to everything in life, a Buddhist gains personal peace and lives in harmony with the world. Buddhists must realize that there are people in the world who get ahead through evil means. We must press the Buddhist: "What is goodness? How do we know what is good?" Moral law points to a moral Lawgiver, namely the true God.

Bridge #5

For the Buddhist, ultimate reality is within the human self. But for the Christian, ultimate reality is in the absolute truth of a God who is outside of human beings. For the Buddhist, reality is thoroughly subjective and inner; for the Christian, it is objective and God-centered. Ultimate reality is revealed only through Jesus Christ, who said, "I am the way, the truth, and the life; no one comes to the Father but through Me" (John 14:6). This is ultimately the choice the Buddhist must make—is it self, or is it Christ?

Reaching the Buddhist with the gospel of Jesus Christ can be difficult. These suggested bridges can be used by the Holy Spirit to pierce the heart of the Buddhist. Both Buddhists and Christians use the metaphor of light to describe the path to truth. A Buddhist journeys into himself for the purpose of negating himself to achieve enlightenment. The Christian journeys into Jesus Christ, the light of the world, to find true enlightenment. That is the message we must take to the Buddhist.

FOR FURTHER DISCUSSION

1. Why is Buddhism considered more of a philosophy than a religion?
2. In what ways did Siddhartha Buddha seek to find life's meaning? In what ways do you see people today searching for meaning?

3. What is your reaction to the Four Noble Truths and the Eightfold Path? What do you see as the positives and negatives of this view of suffering?

4. Review the theology of Buddhism. Why do you think many Westerners find these beliefs appealing?

5. What are the similarities and differences between Hindu theology and Buddhist theology?

6. What did the author mean by the statement, "Fundamentally, Buddhism is an ethical religion?"

7. Which bridge do you see as the most compelling one for the Buddhist? Why? How will you use it?

5

Confucianism

THERE IS NO DOUBT that Confucius is *the* religious figure of importance in China. His influence was not only religious; it was political and practical as well. Politically, Confucius promoted an ethic that would harmonize all human relationships, especially in the government. That ethic had practical application in its support of family relationships. Even today the influence of Confucius remains strong in that nation; in fact, one cannot really understand the Chinese people without understanding Confucianism. This chapter will detail who Confucius was, summarize his teachings, and suggest ways to reach the Chinese Confucianist with the gospel.

Confucius lies at the very center of Chinese culture. Philosopher Lin Yutang has observed:

> To Western readers Confucius is chiefly known as a wise man speaking in aphorisms, five moral axioms, which hardly suffices to explain the depth of influence of Confucius. Without a deeper unity of belief or system of thought, no mere collection of aphorisms could dominate a nation's history as Confucius has dominated China.[1]

The core idea of Confucianism is the concept of virtue, of right living. More than any other major world religion, Confucianism is an attempt to provide systematic order to all human relationships. The Confucian worldview considers justice and happiness for both individuals and for society the highest goals to achieve.

CONFUCIANISM: ITS HISTORY

Life of Confucius

His real name was K'ung Fu-tzu, and he was born in 551 B.C. His father died when he was three, leaving the family poor. At a young age,

Confucius cultivated his lifelong love of poetry and immersed himself in the historical traditions of China. According to the autobiographical summary in his *Analects,* at fifteen he determined to be a scholar. Confucius married at age nineteen, and a year later his only son was born. The government placed him in charge of the state granaries and of public lands in his province. The state also appointed him magistrate of his province and later minister of works and minister of justice.

Confucius never stopped studying the ancient works of China. In fact, he became both an authority on Chinese antiquity and a teacher in addition to his governmental duties. Increasingly, his interest shifted to reforming the government and the society. This concern forced him to reflect on the nature of political authority. What makes a good ruler? His writings and his teachings reflect this desire for reform.[2]

The Influence of Ancient China

The China of Confucius's time was one of political instability, plague, and famine. The ruling dynasty—the Chou dynasty—was in decline and could no longer control the entire country. Religiously, China was an aggregate of animism, polytheism, and ancestral worship. Confucius took the ancient teachings of China and reformulated them into a coherent ethical system of thought.

What were some of these ancient ideas that captivated Confucius and which he attempted to synthesize? First, the core of the Chinese religious conviction is the belief that the world of man and the world of nature are inseparable and interdependent. Beyond that interdependence lies the Eternal Order of the universe, called the *Tao* (pronounced "Dow"). Tao means road, way, or path, but to the Chinese it is the cosmic principle responsible for the harmony and order of nature. Because of the orderliness and cosmic harmony of the Tao, the individual must always seek to conform himself to that orderliness and harmony. Therefore, the natural world is the greatest reflection of the orderliness of the Tao. As Laurence G. Thompson argues, the Tao "might be likened to the Laws of Nature, or better to Nature itself. And whether taken as Being or as Nonbeing, or as the Principle in all particular things, it is in any case *never* conceived as Deity."[3]

The second principle is *Shang Ti*. Shang means "upper" and Ti means "ruler." This "ruler on high" was an ancestral figure type, located in the higher regions of the sky. Later in history, Shang Ti was thought to reside in "heaven" (or the Chinese term *T'ien*).[4]

The third principle is the *Yin-Yang* precept. The Yin-Yang is traced back to the oldest Chinese classic, *The I Ching (Book of Change)*, and is depicted as a symbol found in Western jewelry today (a circle with two "eyes" separated by an S-like figure). In ancient Chinese history, people believed that all natural phenomena operated in accord with and were subject to the control of the Eternal Order, or Tao, which functioned in an interaction of opposing forces of Yin and Yang. The following chart summarizes these opposites, which, when combined, produce order and harmony.

Yang	Yin
Heaven	Earth
Masculine	Feminine
Active	Passive
Warm	Cold
Dry	Wet
Bright	Dark
Positive	Negative

Not only is everything in nature either Yin or Yang, but this principle affects everything in life. In the unseen spirit world, there are good spirits (Yang) and evil spirits (Yin). An elaborate system of pseudo-science developed within Chinese culture to control all parts of nature. The Yin-Yang principle carried over into the ethical world too. Yang is identified with virtue and Yin with vice.[5]

A final principle was that of *divination,* discerning will and direction from mysterious practices. Thompson[6] argues that Chinese divination is motivated by the desire to understand the operations of the natural and supernatural forces in nature, so that one's actions would be in accord with those forces and produce good results. One of the best examples of this type of divination is *feng-shui,* which means "wind and water." When choosing the best site to build a home, for example, people use *feng-shui* to guarantee wealth, prosperity, and honor to those who dwell there.

Divination was also used to keep in touch with deceased family members and help them in the afterlife. The practice of ancestor worship is one specific distinguishing characteristic of the Chinese family, even today. Ancestor worship reinforced the cohesion of the family and its lineage. It was likewise the one universal religious institution throughout China, connecting everyone to family and community. The Chinese have believed for thousands of years that the soul survives death and that there is ongoing contact between the dead and the living. The living family members offer sacrifices and other forms of divination to make the ancestors happy in hopes of receiving their blessing.

The Confucian Texts

The main texts of Confucianism, which form the basis for this faith, have come to us through the disciples of Confucius. Their recollections and interpretations are found in the *Four Books:*[7]

1. The *Analects* (the "Lun Yu"), a collection of the sayings of Confucius and some of his disciples. Though often fragmentary and perplexing, it is the most nearly contemporary document of Confucius we have, with verbatim quotations from the master himself.

2. The *Great Learning* ("Ta Hsueh") dates from a century and a half after Confucius's death and thematically focuses on the ordering of society through the individual's self-cultivation. Originally developed as the basis of education for the "ideal man" in classical Chinese education, it was the first text studied.

3. The *Doctrine of the Mean* ("Chung Yung") is an excellent exposition of the philosophical presuppositions of Confucianism and relates human nature to the underlying moral order of the universe.

4. The *Book of Mencius*, dating from the third century B.C., is a collection of the writings and sayings of the most original of the early Confucian thinkers. Mencius has been called "the St. Paul to Confucius."

CONFUCIANISM AS A WORLDVIEW: ITS THEOLOGY AND ITS ETHICS

God: Confucius's teaching on heaven and God is not religious; Confucius did not see God as personal and infinite. He once said, "Absorption in the study of the supernatural is most harmful."[8] Confucianism is a humanistic, this-worldly, rational, ethical teaching that has dominated the thought and action of the Chinese people for centuries.

Humanity: Confucius taught that humans are born essentially, innately, and morally good. How is a human to cultivate this innate goodness? For Confucius it meant following the Tao ("the way") to become the "ideal (or superior) man" ("chun-tzu"). As intrinsic goodness is cultivated, it overflows into the common life to serve the state and all humans.

The Confucian concept of the ideal man encompasses five major virtues and five major social relationships. The five virtues are (compared to the parts of a tree):

• *Jen*—Mutual benevolence, the will to seek the good of others (the root)
• *Yi*—Righteousness by justice (the trunk)
• *Li*—Propriety or reverence (the branches)
• *Chih*—Wisdom (the flower)
• *Hsin*—Faithfulness/Faith (the fruit)[9]

The ideal man is the embodiment of *Jen* (pronounced "ren"), which is the internal motivation to fulfill the other virtues. Because one is benevolent, one will manifest justice (*Yi*) and propriety (*Li*) in external relationships so that wisdom (*Chih*) and faithfulness (*Hsin*) will be the dominant character traits. Confucius wrote, "Desiring to sustain oneself, one sustains others; desiring to develop oneself, one develops others."[10] For that reason, the ideal man will always follow the Doctrine of the Mean: "Not to do to others what you do not wish yourself."

For Confucianism, there are five major social relationships demonstrating that the ideal man relates well to his family and extends his virtues to society at large. Those cardinal relationships and corresponding virtues look like this:

Relationship	Virtue
sovereign to subject	faithful loyalty
father to son	filial piety
elder to younger brother	fraternity
husband to wife	fidelity
friend to friend	friendly reciprocity

The family is the basic unit of society, and the ideal man recognizes that. He also understands that the ideal society is one in which all citizens know their proper place and their respective virtues.[11]

Because man is innately good, Confucius envisioned a utopian society where the ruler would benevolently rule as he followed the Doctrine of the Mean, seeking to become an ideal man. His subordinates would each seek to become the ideal man as well. This trickle-down ethic would have this effect:

First, extend to the utmost their knowledge in the investigation of things (antiquity). As a result knowledge will be complete which will in turn cause thoughts to become sincere. With thoughts sincere, the heart will be rectified. With the heart right, the person will be cultivated. With the person cultivated, the family will be regulated. With the family regulated, the government will be right and the whole empire will be made tranquil and happy.[12]

If Confucius is correct that humans are predisposed to goodness, his scheme is possible. If humans are not predisposed to goodness, his scheme collapses into meaningless individual autonomy.

Ancestor Worship: In many ways, the basic religion of China remains ancestor worship. The teachings of Confucius gave ethical meaning to this practice. Because his ethical system begins with the family, he consistently taught that parents must be treated with total respect. He instructed children to stay close to parents, especially when they became elderly. Love for parents is a lifetime commitment that continues even after their death. For Confucius, the most pious acts included repairing and keeping the ancestral temples orderly, carefully arranging the sacrificial vessels, the regalia, and the heirlooms of the family, and presenting appropriate sacrifices to them.[13]

Heaven: According to the Doctrine of the Mean, Confucius taught that the truths handed down from the ancients "harmonize with the divine order which governs the revolutions of the seasons in the Heaven above and . . . fit in with the moral design which is to be seen in physical nature upon the Earth below."[14] It seems that Confucius believed that his teaching had heaven's sanction and carried eternal significance because the teaching had its origin in the moral order of the world. However, there is no sense in the Confucian worldview of the personal God to whom Christians pray and relate. Heaven in Confucius's mind is not where a sovereign personal God dwells. Heaven is a divine principle synonymous with the eternal order of things. Heaven manifests the Tao of the universe.

The Cult of Confucius: The elevation and worship of Confucius began between the second and first centuries B.C. when the emperors honored him as a great sage and began to worship and make sacrifices at his grave. (One emperor sacrificed an ox, a sheep, and a pig.) By the second century A.D., readings, prayers, and gifts of money and silk were added to the sacrifices at the grave. In A.D. 630 the Chinese emperor issued a decree obliging every governor of China to erect a state temple to Confucius in which regular sacrifices to him were ordered. About a hundred years later, another emperor placed images of Confucius in the great hall of the state temples.[15]

In the beginning of the twentieth century, the Manchu rulers wanted to make Confucianism the main religion of China. Dr. Sun Yat-sen (1866-1925), founder of the Chinese republic, continued to revere Confucius and tie his teaching to the new nation. Chiang Kai-shek centered his leadership of the Chinese Nationalists (now living in Taiwan) on the revised teachings of Confucius. Despite Mao Tse-tung's (1893-1976) attempt to destroy Confucianism and replace it with communism, it is evident since his death that many Chinese people continue to affirm the basic tenets of Confucianism.[16]

BUILDING BRIDGES TO THE CONFUCIANIST

Bridge #1

The Chinese ideal for society and for personal peace and happiness is to achieve order and harmony. There is an intense search for harmony in human relationships in Chinese thinking. The problem for the Chinese worldview so deeply rooted in the ancient texts including Confucianism is that it searches for order and harmony without any personal God, the author of such order and harmony. Christianity is likewise interested in the order and harmony of the family and society. That love for order and harmony is rooted in the personal, transcendent, and infinite Creator. For the Christian, right actions—a concept extremely important to the Chinese—are attained by aligning oneself with God's revealed righteousness in Jesus Christ.

Bridge #2

The Chinese worldview, rooted in the ancient texts and Confucianism, focuses strongly on the family. Confucius taught the perpetual respect and honor for parents and ancestors. The impact of the extended family is central to understanding the Chinese mind. Christianity affirms the critical importance of the family too—the first institution God created (see Gen. 2). The New Testament teachings of order, structure, love respect, and honor within the family are fundamental to Christianity (see Eph. 5:22ff.). Both the Christian and the Confucian worldview embrace the importance of family, and it can be common ground between them.

Bridge #3

The Confucian worldview has a high regard for personal and social ethics, the foundation of the Confucian system. The five major virtues and the five major relationships emphasize this point. The Doctrine of the Mean in Confucianism is identical to the teaching of Jesus (Matt. 7:12). Christians must therefore live authentic lives. Ethical commitment to honesty, truth, and justice are important to the Chinese and are valuable to Christians because they reflect the attributes of almighty God. This commonality of interest in personal and social ethics can provide a powerful and compelling bridge to share the truth about Jesus.

The entire Chinese way of life is now being challenged. Materialism, pluralism, Western culture, and the abandonment of ideological communism have left a spiritual and moral vacuum among the Chinese people. We have a fantastic opportunity to reach out to these people, located on every continent, with the truth of Jesus Christ. Rural life in mainland China is quickly fading as the urban centers grow and adapt to a quasi-capitalism. The Christian church in China is growing and with it the opportunity to confront the Chinese with the claims of Christ.

FOR FURTHER DISCUSSION

1. Why was Confucius more than simply a wise man with profound sayings?
2. Explain the relationship between the ideas of Tao and Yin-Yang. Is this view of order and harmony consistent with a Christian view of the world? Why or why not?
3. Imagine that God and heaven were merely impersonal principles. How would you feel? How would this affect your daily life and faith?
4. In what ways is the theology of Confucianism similar to the theology of naturalism (chapter 2)?
5. What is the Bible's concept of an ideal human being? How does this differ from the Confucian concept of the ideal man?
6. Debate this statement by Confucius about one's internal motivation to virtue: "Desiring to sustain oneself, one sustains others."
7. Name some additional bridges that could be used to reach Confucianists.

6

Shintoism

WHEN MILITANT NATIONALISTS ruled Japan during the first half of the twentieth century, Shintoism was the official state religion of the country. It venerated the uniqueness of Japanese culture and bestowed divinity on the emperor. Soldiers who gave their lives for their country were quasi-deities, their souls honored in Shinto shrines, especially the large Yasukuni Shrine near the Imperial Palace in Tokyo. For many Japanese people, state Shintoism and military imperialism were inextricably linked. After World War II, Emperor Hirohito renounced his divinity, Shinto lost its official protection, and the new Constitution upheld the principle of church-state separation. However, Shintoism retains a special defining power in Japanese civilization.

According to Shintoism, Japan's national character was formed before history was recorded. When Japan was born, the emperor was already a high priest and head of state. He was a descendant in an unbroken line from the sun-goddess Amaterasu. The imperial family, therefore, cannot be separated from Japanese mythology. The myths chronicle the birth of Japan. The emperor is sacred because his blood ties go back to the gods who created the nation. Shintoism provides Japan with the spiritual culture central to its identity. For that reason when Emperor Hirohito died in 1989, the funeral ceremony contained all the trappings of Shintoism. As the ancient Shinto rituals were performed, national and international leaders gathered at the Grand Shrine at Ise in central Japan. Today Shintoism still defines the "who" and "what" of the Japanese people and their culture.[1]

About 90 percent of the people of Japan identify themselves as Shinto followers, although about 75 percent of that 90 percent also identify themselves as Buddhists. (Less than 1 percent of Japan is Christian.) For many in Japan, there is no conflict in saying they belong to both religions. We have already discussed Buddhism; what exactly is

Shintoism? What are its distinctives? Although ancient, why does it still define Japanese civilization?

SHINTOISM: ITS HISTORY

The term "Shinto" is derived from the Chinese *shentao*, meaning "the way of the higher spirits or gods." To understand Shintoism, one must understand the concept of *kami*; Shinto is the way of kami. The term captures the transcendent element that affects all nature and life. Kami includes the various deities of heaven and earth, all forms of life—human, animal, and vegetable—as well as all things dreaded and revered. Kami refers to beings that possess sacred power or superior potency, filled with charismatic power. Kami is the single most important aspect of Japanese Shintoism.[2]

The origin of the doctrine of kami is rooted deep in Japanese history. Part of Japanese mythology recounts that Japan was once peopled exclusively with kami. The early Japanese regarded the whole of nature—mountains, lakes, trees, sea, and ground—as having kami powers. Shinto belief thus expresses a religious faith about Japan and its past. The customs of prehistoric Japan were the way followed by kami, the beings from whom the Japanese people are descended.[3]

The introduction of Buddhism and Confucianism into Japan, largely during the A.D. 700s, changed Shinto beliefs. These influences resulted in the systematized Shintoism that became a national religion. The ethics of Confucius introduced a new moral character into the kami and into religious practices as well. The Japanese adopted ancestor worship as a part of kami worship, stressing the important influence of genealogical descent of the kami. Confucian thought also influenced the social stratification of society into a ruling class and a common class. Buddhism became a religion of the upper class while the common people held to the veneration of their regional kami.[4]

In A.D. 710, the Japanese capital was moved from Yamato to Nara, beginning the Nara and Heian Periods of Japanese history (710-1191). Using the newly acquired Chinese writing skills, court scribes began to record the oral traditions of the Shinto mythologies. There are four major writings of importance. The *Kojiki* ("Chronicle of Ancient Events"), completed in 712, is the major history of mythology explaining the origin of the cosmos, the Japanese islands, the people, and the divine descendence of the emperor. The *Fudo-Ki* (713) is a topographical record that lists all the shrines and the oral tradition behind the kami manifestations that occurred at each shrine. The *Nihonshiki* ("Chronicles of Japan"), completed in 720, is a historical account of the ruling court from Japan's beginning. Finally, the *Engishiki* (927) is a compendium of Shinto traditions consisting of fifty parts. The most important is the *Norito*, the model for prayers at the Shinto shrines. [5]

It was also during the Nara and Heian periods that the government used these various writings to tie the nation and the official court to the past mythology of the ancient kami veneration. Finally, during these periods the government used the term "Shinto," which was defined as "the kami way."

By the 1100s, a mixture of Shinto and Buddhist practices had developed. The government began to build Shinto and Buddhist shrines side by side. The royal court put its stamp of approval upon Buddhism but also maintained the distinctive Shinto faith and practice. New Buddhist schools emerged that stressed the coexistence of Shinto and Buddhism in Buddhist terms. This mixture of Shinto and Buddhist beliefs and practices continued for several centuries.[6]

In 1868 the religious climate of Japan changed dramatically. Emperor Meiji made Shinto the state religion and ordered the elimination of Buddhism. The ancient view of the divine origin and authority of the emperor was again promoted within a state Shinto system consisting of government-sponsored programs. World War II shattered the unique Japanese faith in the inviolability and divine origin of their island, people, and emperor. Shintoism and Buddhism survive in Japan today, but the mythological mysticism of Shintoism has lost some of its former power.[7]

SHINTOISM AS A WORLDVIEW: ITS THEOLOGY AND ETHICS

In Japanese religious history, Shintoism is unique to the Japanese islands. Shinto refers to the traditional practices that originated in Japan and developed mainly among the Japanese people. There are no clearly defined doctrines, codes of behavior, specific canon, nor a specific founder of the faith.

In analyzing Shintoism, it is necessary to define the six major types:

1. *Domestic Shinto.* This type refers to the rituals performed at homes rather than at communal shrines. In the homes there are *kami-*

dana, or "god-shelves," on which are placed memorial tablets with the names of long-honored ancestors or perhaps a patron deity of the household written on them. Ancestor worship plays a significant role in domestic Shinto.

2. *Folk Shinto.* This type encompasses local Shinto varieties found throughout the Japanese islands.

3. *Imperial Household Shinto.* This includes the special rites followed by the Imperial family at shrines within the Imperial Palace.

4. *State Shinto.* Historically, this was the most important and influential type of Shintoism. It was a government-fostered program of patriotic rites conducted from the 1860s through 1945 at the national shrines. Observed at the more than 110,000 national shrines existing before World War II, the ceremonies were to cultivate national patriotism and "the spirit of ancient Japan." The American occupation of Japan after the war ended the compulsory aspects of state Shintoism. Many of the state shrines were abolished or fell into disuse.

5. *Shrine Shinto.* Supported by private funds and voluntary gifts, many of these 110,000 shrines were rebuilt or renovated. Shrine Shinto refers to the core of traditional religious practices centered in rites related to these various shrines.

6. *Sect Shinto.* Various sectarian or religious Shintoists have emerged in the modern history of Japan. They vary widely in their importance, but each relates to Shinto beliefs and practices in some way.[8]

Kami: Since the concept of kami is so central to Shintoism, it is necessary to define this clearly. It is an abstract term; the English word *god* is not accurate. The basic idea of kami is "above" or "superior." Anything awe-inspiring may be "kamified" (e.g., the sun, wind, thunder, mountains). Today, kami refers to spiritual beings, mythological entities of ancient times, natural phenomena, physical objects of worship, or ancestral spirits.[9]

Creation: Shintoists recognize a creation of heaven and earth as a spontaneous generation of an original trio of kami deities. The first Japanese emperor was an offspring of the gods. The Japanese islands are also a special creation of the gods.[10]

Ethics: There is no written ethical code in Shintoism nor are there clearly defined standards in the Shinto faith. There are no absolutes; rather good is associated with beauty, conformity, excellence, nobility, and so on. Human beings are viewed as innately good, but purification rites are required if a person is defiled through contact with blood, sickness, or death. The purification is purely external; there is no reference to internal cleansing from sin as in Christianity or Judaism.[11]

Worship: Shinto worship focuses on certain rites or traditional practices at the various shrines, whether in the home or at the regional or national shrines. Here the kami or symbolic representations of the kami are enshrined. The shrine is the center of Shinto worship and supplies an abode for the kami. There are no images to worship in the shrine; kami may be known or unknown by the worshiper. Each part of Japan has a shrine dedicated to the local kami. Worship involves purification to rid oneself of impurities before approaching the kami.

There are also offerings to the kami, which include rice, water, salt, fish, or other foods. At communal shrines, the worshiper often gives money. Prayers are an aspect of worship, but they are often not verbal; rather, they might involve a sense of communion with the kami. Worship involves the sacred meal. Here the worshiper fellowships with the kami with whom the meal is symbolically shared. Finally, worship includes festivals and ceremonies. Every shrine has a festival day in which the entire community joins in celebration. Festivals consist of eating, drinking, dancing, and entertainment. Most shrine festivals are no longer celebrated in Japan, but there are two exceptions. During the fall, the Harvest Festival is overseen by the emperor, and twice a year the Great Purification Ceremony takes place to cleanse the nation of its impurities.[12]

BUILDING BRIDGES TO THE SHINTOIST

When one views Japan today, one sees a nation undergoing intense transition. World War II destroyed state Shintoism, but the other types mentioned continue. Overall, Shintoism is declining; emperor worship is dead and Buddhism lacks appeal to the typical Japanese person today. There remains the strong emphasis on the family and communal commitment. The nation is also economically prosperous. Corporate success in the urban areas appears to be the basic goal of the individual. In rural Japan, Shintoism lingers, but its power is declining. Many parts of Japanese civilization reflect a religious vacuum.

Christianity has a most negative reputation in Japan. It was brought to Japan in 1549 by Francis Xavier, but it has not grown successfully. It was banned until the mid-1840s. Today less than 1 percent of the Japanese population affirms Christianity.

Bridge #1

Shintoism promotes the importance of the family and the community; so does Christianity. Both see the family as strategic to the larger civilization. Both understand the importance of honor and respect in family relationships and in the larger community.

Bridge #2

Because Shintoism is highly pragmatic, it is important to stress the practical benefits of Christianity. Christianity provides a reason for existence. Because the Japanese appreciate the importance of community, a loving, committed, friendly church can provide a strong, loving, and committed fellowship. An authentic, functioning New Testament church can be appealing to the Japanese.

Bridge #3

Because honor is such a core value of Shintoism, Christianity offers the basis for honoring all human beings—they are made in the image of God. This concept is somewhat close to the idea of kami and can be a strong connecting point for Christianity.

Japanese Shinto culture is very difficult to penetrate. Part of this difficulty is due to the fact that Shinto worship does not promote morality and ethics. The Japanese Shinto culture has no religious or philosophical basis. This deficiency is heightened by the materialism and prosperity of modern Japanese culture. There is a real spiritual vacuum within Japanese society today. The country is Western in its economic orientation and increasingly in its cultural orientation.

From the outside, Japanese culture is heavily influenced by American pop culture and by the materialism that goes with it. Yet Japan keeps the traditions of Shintoism, although with decreasing commitment by many of the young people. So for this next generation there may be an openness to Christianity that has never characterized Japan. Shintoism no longer works and Western culture and materialism do not provide the organizing purpose and center for civilization. Japanese civilization is very vulnerable right now. Perhaps God will use this unique moment to pour out His Holy Spirit. Let us pray and work toward that end.

For Further Discussion

1. Define "Shinto" and "kami." Why are these important to Shintoism?
2. How did Emperor Meiji change Shintoism as he aligned the religion more with the state?
3. Describe the following types of Shintoism:
   - Domestic Shinto
   - State Shintoism
   - Shrine Shintoism
4. How did the Japanese defeat in World War II change Shintoism? How does this change underscore the problems with viewing nations and humans as divine?
5. Summarize the following aspects of the Shinto worldview:
   - creation
   - ethics
   - worship
6. Discuss the dangers of a society based on material prosperity. What is the best way to penetrate this type of culture with the gospel? Spend time praying for the spiritual state of Shintoists.
7. The author suggests three bridges we as Christians can build to reach the Japanese Shintoist. Name some possible additional bridges to Shintoism.

7

Judaism

IN JUNE 1987 the Reverend Bailey Smith, former president of the Southern Baptist Convention, audaciously declared that "God Almighty doesn't hear the prayer of a Jew," resulting in a veritable firestorm of criticism from both Christians and Jews. But Smith's comments reflect the tension Christians often feel when confronting Judaism. Christianity was born out of Judaism. Jesus and Paul, for example, were both Jews. But the fundamental difference separating the Christian from the Jew today remains the Messiahship of Jesus: Christians believe He is the Messiah; Jews do not. This gap between the two is seemingly insurmountable.

That gap between Christians and Jews over Jesus is compounded by the realities of history. The early church, clearly Jewish, was successful in reaching out to Gentiles, which in turn led to the landmark ruling of the Jerusalem Council (Acts 15). That decision in A.D. 49 released Gentile converts from the necessity of circumcision and adherence to the Mosaic law. By championing the cause of Gentile freedom from Jewish rituals and regulations, Paul and other apostolic leaders in effect produced a new community of believers. Could Jew and Gentile Christian live harmoniously together? As the second century dawned, this harmony became more problematic. Another point of contention between Jew and Christian (both Gentile and Jewish Christians) involved moving worship on the Sabbath to the Lord's Day.

Finally, the growing persecution of Jews widened the split between Christian and Jew. During the two early Jewish revolts against Rome (A.D. 66-73 and 132-135), Jewish Christians refused to fight, compromising both their allegiance to the Jewish community and their identity with the early Jewish state. Further, the destruction of Jerusalem in A.D. 70 and the disappearance of all major Jewish sects but the Pharisees forced a reformulation of Judaism. Rabbinic Judaism, as the new form came to be called, emerged as a separate religion from Christianity, and the deep-seated rivalry between synagogue and church developed. That institutional split remains today.[1]

The tearing away from Jewish roots resulted in the church defining itself largely in non-Jewish terminology. The term "Christianity" is an obvious example, for it gives singular focus to Jesus as the Christ (Greek) or the Messiah (Hebrew). The name of Christianity's holy book, the Bible, is a Greek term, a signal that this new faith was stepping away from Judaism. In addition, by the third century the early church had taken on an increasingly anti-Jewish tone. The posture of early Christian writings was decidedly against the synagogue system. Whereas one Gentile nation after another responded positively to the Christian message, Jews continued to cling stubbornly to their ancestral faith. The later leaders of the church taught that the unfaithfulness of the Jewish people resulted in a collective guilt that made them subject to the permanent curse of God. As church history progressed, contempt grew for the Jews and Judaism.

In the fourth century, when Emperor Constantine made Christianity a legitimate religion of Rome, Jews experienced a further wave of discrimination and persecution. They lost many of their legal rights, including being expelled from Jerusalem. In 339 it was considered a criminal offense to convert to Judaism.

During the medieval period (A.D. 500 to 1500), Jews were largely excluded from Christian culture. Therefore, Jews often avoided the Christian culture in Europe by living in secluded parts of the cities. Jews engaged in one major profession—money-lending. Deprived of basic liberties and ostracized from the culture, Jews were required to wear a distinctive hat or to sew a patch on their clothing. The Christian culture blamed Jews for many social wrongs but especially of being "Christ-killers." During the 1490s, the Spanish Inquisition persecuted Jews and eventually ordered them to leave Spain. Because they were not permitted to enter Western Europe, they fled to North Africa, Morocco, and the Eastern Mediterranean.

This ruthless persecution of Jews across Europe, including most viciously in czarist Russia, caused over two million to flee to America. But the Holocaust stands as the unparalleled embodiment of anti-Semitism's horror. The final solution of the Nazis involved concentration camps, gas chambers, and crematoriums. Between 1933, when Hitler came to power, and the end of World War II (1945), some six million Jews were exterminated. Wherever Jews are today, a vestige of anti-Semitism remains.[2]

JUDAISM: ITS HISTORY

In a world of more than 6.2 billion people, there are only 17 million Jews. Yet their impact on world history and on religious truth has been profound. The history of Judaism is the Old Testament. Jews are called "Hebrews," from Eber mentioned in Genesis 10:21. They are also descended from one of Noah's sons, Shem, from which the term "Semitic" originates. But Abraham is the true father of the Jewish people.

Abraham, a descendant of Shem (Gen. 11:10-28), lived in Mesopotamia, in the town of Ur around 2000 B.C. According to Genesis 12:1-7, the true God spoke to him and instructed him to leave Ur and go to a land that He would give him. God made (literally "cut") a covenant with Abraham, promising him that he would be the father of an entire nation of peoples, whose numbers would compare with the sand of the seashore and the stars of the sky. In addition, in Abraham all of the nations would be blessed. Finally, God promised Abraham and his descendants land—the land of Palestine (Gen. 12:8; 17:8). In essence, the covenant promise was land, seed, and blessing.

Abraham's son Isaac was the covenant son promised by God. He was born when Abraham was 100 years old, but, when Isaac was a teenager, God asked Abraham to sacrifice the boy to Him on Mount Moriah. In obedience Abraham took his son and was prepared to offer him back to God when God intervened, providing a ram as a substitutionary sacrifice. This test of Abraham's faith proved that he loved God and obeyed Him (Gen. 22). Isaac's covenant son was Jacob, who had twelve sons, the founders of what would become the twelve tribes of Israel (Jacob's covenant name, according to Gen. 32).

One of Jacob's sons, Joseph, was hated by his bothers, sold into slavery, and ended up as prime minister in the Egyptian government. In that role, Joseph provided food for his brothers and their families, bringing them to Egypt in the land of Goshen, in the Nile Delta region (Gen. 37—50). Israel grew into such a formidable nation that the pharaoh of Egypt enslaved them (Ex. 1).

Moses, himself a Hebrew but raised in the pharaoh's court, became the "deliverer" of the Israelites from their 400 years of slavery in Egypt. In confronting the pharaoh, Moses declared that the God of Israel was the true God, and He would prove it. That proof was the ten plagues against Egypt, each one directed at a specific Egyptian god. As a result of God's war on the Egyptian gods, the pharaoh allowed the Israelites to leave, carrying much of the wealth of Egypt with them (Ex. 5—14).

To Moses God had revealed Himself as the great "I AM THAT I AM," the self-sufficient, self-existent Being of the universe (Ex. 3:14). Moses, a highly educated and brilliant man, recorded the early history of the Israelites in the first five books of the Old Testament (called the Torah or the Pentateuch). In that history, Genesis 1—11 declares that God created the physical world, cursed it for its sinful rebellion, and scattered the peoples throughout the world. He promised that He would redeem His creation through the "seed of the woman" (Gen. 3:15).

Under Moses' understudy, Joshua, the Israelites conquered the land of Palestine (Canaan), which God had promised to Abraham (recorded in the book of Joshua). Then they organized the land administratively in a decentralized manner (see the book of Judges). After the failure of the Judges, the people demanded a king like the surrounding nations. God granted that request, and after the reign of Saul, David became the king of Israel (about 1000 B.C.).

Under David Israel became a great nation. He consolidated his power, vanquished Israel's enemies, and made Jerusalem the capital city. David desired to build a mighty temple dedicated to the God of Israel, but because he was a man of war, God prohibited it. Instead, God promised David an eternal dynasty, throne, and kingdom (2 Sam. 7:16). From that covenant promise comes the promise of an anointed one, or Messiah, from God.

After David's son Solomon built the temple and established Israel as a wealthy military power, the kingdom of Israel split apart as a result of sin and rebellion; Israel was the northern kingdom, and Judah was in the south. After Solomon, Israel was ruled by a series of kings who did not honor God; only a few God-honoring kings came to power in Judah. God warned both Israel and Judah of impending judgment through his prophets (most of those warnings are recorded in the major prophets [e.g., Isaiah, Jeremiah, etc.] and the minor prophets [e.g., Joel, Amos, Hosea, etc.] in the Old Testament). As He said He would, God judged Israel for its idolatry and disobedience first through its conquest by Assyria in 722 B.C. The people of Israel were taken from the land in the north and relocated, never to return as a united people to their land. God judged Judah for its idolatry and disobedience in 586 B.C.

Nebuchadnezzar of Babylonia successfully conquered the nation, destroyed the temple, and took most of the people back to Babylonia. (These events are recorded in the biblical books of 1 and 2 Kings and 1 and 2 Chronicles.)

The Jews of the Babylonian exile returned to their land seventy years later (recorded in Ezra and Nehemiah) and rebuilt the wall and the temple. They remained in their land until they rebelled against Roman occupation in A.D. 66. The Roman Empire responded savagely. Over the next four years, and especially during the siege of Jerusalem in A.D. 70, thousands of Jews were slaughtered (many by crucifixion), the city was razed, the temple was destroyed, and the remaining Jews were dispersed throughout the world. Their sacrificial system, their priestly worship, and their identity as a people with a nation ended.

After the return from the Babylonian exile, various sects of Judaism emerged. Each had a distinctive emphasis, and each played a role in the development of Judaism.

The Sadducees. Originally a party of aristocratic, wealthy leaders, the Sadducees accommodated their beliefs to the changing culture of Judea. They separated themselves from popular teaching and focused on the rational, easily defined teaching of the Torah only ("The Books of Moses"). They rejected the popular belief in angels and bodily resurrection, and they embraced the rationalism of Greco-Roman culture.

The Pharisees. The Pharisees consisted of the scribes, the rabbis, and most of the priesthood of Judaism. They adhered to the oral tradition that accompanied the Torah, the expositions, interpretations, and commentaries of the scribes and rabbis. Pharisees embraced the doctrine of the bodily resurrection, the last judgment of God at the end of history, and devotion to God's law. They scrupulously studied the Scriptures and rabbinic "tradition," stressing moral obedience, ceremonial purity, prayers, fasting, and the giving of alms to the poor. They were the legalists of Jewish society.

The Essenes. Although other parties emerged in Judaism at this time (e.g., the Herodians, who accommodated to Rome's rule, and the Zealots, revolutionaries who desired to overthrow Rome), the Essenes withdrew from Judean society to prepare for Messiah's coming. They lived in monastic seclusion where they fasted and prayed, following ceremonial rituals. The Essenes were the Jewish group that inhabited Qumran, where the famous Dead Sea Scrolls were discovered decades ago.[3]

JUDAISM AS A WORLDVIEW: ITS THEOLOGY AND ETHICS

With the destruction of the temple, the sacrificial system, and the priests in A.D. 70, the focal point of Judaism was the Law. The entire body of written and oral tradition of Judaism is known as "Torah," which "represents to the Jew the whole mystery and tangible expression of God."[4] The debates, discussions, and decisions of scholars and rabbis on the meaning of Torah were eventually compiled into a monumental work called the "Talmud," which aids the Jew in making the connection between theology and life.

Throughout Jewish history, there has been little focus on articulating a creed or confession of belief. The most significant attempt to do so was that of the twelfth century Jewish teacher, Moses Maimonides, who listed thirteen articles. This list remains a part of the Authorized Prayer Book.[5]

1. Belief in the existence of a Creator and Providence.
2. Belief in His unity.
3. Belief in His incorporeality [i.e., not of flesh and blood].
4. Belief in His eternity.
5. Belief that to Him alone is worship due.
6. Belief in the words of the prophets.
7. Belief that Moses was the greatest of all prophets.
8. Belief in the revelation of the Lord to Moses at Sinai.
9. Belief in the immutability of the revealed Law.
10. Belief that God is omniscient.
11. Belief in retribution in this world and the hereafter.
12. Belief in the coming of the Messiah.
13. Belief in the resurrection of the dead.

God: The theological center of Judaism is Deuteronomy 6:4-5: "The LORD (Yahweh) is our God (Elohim); the LORD is one." Jews are to love Him with heart, soul, and strength. God is transcendent (beyond the physical world) and is the Creator of all that exists. He is a God of righteousness, holiness, justice, and love. He deserves singular worship and devotion. He creates humans in His image, which becomes the basis for the value and worth of all humans. Jews teach that God's revelation to humanity in the Old Testament (OT) is how we as creatures know about Him and understand Him.

The Scriptures: Judaism looks at Scripture differently than

Christianity. The Old Testament books remain the center of Jewish Scripture. In fact, between A.D. 69 to 90 a group of Jewish scholars, students, and rabbis gathered in Jamnia, Israel, to finalize what books exactly were in the Old Testament canon. They agreed to group the OT into the Torah (the first five books of the OT), the Prophets (the history books of Joshua, Judges, 1 and 2 Samuel, and 1 and 2 Kings; and the major and minor prophets), and the Miscellaneous books (comprising the rest of the OT books). For most Jews, this is the canon. However, over the history of Judaism other books of importance were added. About A.D. 200 the Mishnah was added, which includes about 4,000 precepts of rabbinic law. About A.D. 500 the Mishnah was combined with the Halakah (oral tradition of the Jewish people with instructions for daily living) and the Haggadah (multiple synagogue homilies) to form the Talmud, a work of some thirty-six volumes.

For Orthodox Jews, not only is the Torah their daily guide for life, but so is the Talmud. They seek to bring their lives into meticulous conformity with both the Torah and the Talmud. Eating procedures are very important to the Orthodox Jew. Pork and shellfish are forbidden in their diet. Animals that are slaughtered for food must be done so in a special "kosher" manner, certified as such by rabbis. Further, Orthodox Jews refrain from working, traveling, using the phone, touching money, or even posing for pictures on the Sabbath. These are just a few of the multiple restrictions detailed in the Talmud.

Conservative and Reform Jews have departed significantly from Orthodox Jewry. Conservative Jews are more lenient in their interpretations of the Law, and Reform Jews teach that principles are more important than Jewish practices. In fact, Reform Jews rarely observe dietary or Sabbath restrictions.[6]

Jewish Customs and Festivals: Within contemporary Judaism, there is widespread agreement on one thing—observance of the Sabbath. For the Jew, the Sabbath begins at sundown on Friday night and continues until sundown Saturday. In Orthodox and some Conservative Jewish homes, as the sun is setting on Friday, the mother (traditionally) lights the designated candles and gives the blessing: "Blessed are Thou, O Lord our God, King of the Universe, Who has sanctified us by Thy laws and commanded us to kindle the Sabbath light." The father then blesses the wine, and everyone takes a sip before the father slices the Sabbath bread.

After the Sabbath dinner, Conservative and Reform families go to the synagogue. For the Orthodox Jew, the main service is on Saturday morning; Orthodox and most Conservatives attend another Saturday service that afternoon.[7]

Judaism has other High Holy Days. Among them are Rosh Hashana (the Jewish New Year celebrated in September or October) and Yom Kippur, the Day of Atonement. These Holy Days are characterized by repentance, prayer, and acts of kindness toward others. This period of self-examination results in open confession and a commitment to abstain from these sins in the year to come. Although the Day of Atonement is wrapped around the OT sacrifice of the lamb that atoned for (covered) sin, the idea of substitutionary sacrifice is lost in much of modern Judaism.[8]

Another significant Jewish High Holy Day is Passover, celebrated approximately the same time as the Christian Easter. Preceded by the Feast of Unleavened Bread (where all leaven is removed from the home), Passover begins with the question from the youngest son, "Why is this night different from all other nights?" An older family member answers, "We were slaves unto pharaoh in Egypt and the Eternal God led us from there with mighty hand." The Passover meal uses a roast shank bone to remind the family of the lamb that was slain and whose blood was sprinkled on the doorposts in Egypt so that the angel of death would recognize Jewish homes and "pass over" them. Today the Passover celebration includes not only prayers and special foods but also games for the children.[9]

When a Jewish boy reaches the age of thirteen, he becomes a "Son of the Commandment (or Covenant)," called a *Barmitzvah*, and is called up for the reading of the Torah on the Sabbath following his birthday. On that occasion, he recites the words: "Blessed are Thou, O Lord our God, King of the Universe, who has chosen us from all peoples, and has given us Thy Torah." Today in some Jewish synagogues, girls go through a similar ceremony called a *Batmitzvah*.[10]

The Messiah: For Jews of the Conservative and Reform perspective, the belief in a coming Messiah who will deliver Israel and bring about the consummation of history is no longer viable. Indeed, for many Jews the rebirth of the modern state of Israel in 1948 is now directly associated with the idea of Messiah. For one of the founders of that state, David Ben Gurion, the Messianic vision is centralized in the establishment of the state: "The ingathering of the exiles, the return of the Jewish people to their land, is the beginning of the realization of the Messianic vision."[11]

This mixing of political and religious ideas is central to understanding Judaism, Messiah, and the modern state of Israel. Thomas Friedman[12] argues that there are four distinct groups of Jews within modern Israel (and the world). The first and largest is the secular and nonobservant Jews who built the modern state of Israel. Many of them are secular Zionists who came to Israel in part as a rebellion against their grandfathers and Orthodox Judaism. For these secular Jews, being in the land, erecting a modern society and army, and observing the Jewish holidays as national holidays all substitute for religious observance and faith.

The second group is the religious Zionists, who are traditional or modern Orthodox Jews who fully support the secular Zionist state but insist it is not a substitute for the synagogue. The creation of the Jewish state is a religious, "messianic" event.

The third group is the religious or messianic Zionists who see the rebirth of the Jewish state as the first stage in a process that will culminate with the coming of the Messiah. The state is the necessary instrument for bringing the Messiah. Every inch of the land of Israel must be settled, and all defense and foreign policies are devoted to this end.

The final group is the ultra-Orthodox, non-Zionist Jews who do not regard the Jewish state as important. Only when the personal Messiah returns, and the rule of Jewish law is complete will the true Jewish state be created.[13]

Therefore, Jews today reject the teaching that Jesus is the Messiah. Except among the ultra-Orthodox and some messianic Zionists, the idea of a personal Messiah who will return to bring about a kingdom of peace, righteousness, and justice is foreign. The Messiah idea is either politicized and associated with the modern state of Israel or rejected as an aspect of an antiquated belief of a dead form of Judaism.

BUILDING BRIDGES TO JUDAISM

Because there is so much historical connection between Judaism and Christianity, the only significant bridge is Jesus. As mentioned above, most Jews reject the teaching that Jesus is the Messiah. The Christian must build the case that He indeed is Messiah. How can that be accomplished?

First, it is important to connect key New Testament (NT) passages with key Old Testament prophecies. Some examples include clear NT references to Jesus as the Messiah (or Christ)—see Matthew 16:16; 26:63-65; Luke 24:26; John 8:28. Also, when King Herod wanted to know where the Christ would be born, his advisors quoted Micah 5:1-3 for the answer—Bethlehem, the very city where Jesus was born. Matthew connects Isaiah's prophecy of 7:14 with the birth of Jesus (Matt. 1:23). Zechariah 9:9 clearly states that Messiah will come humbly, riding on a donkey into Jerusalem. That is what Jesus did on Palm Sunday (Matt. 21:4). Most study Bibles have charts that demonstrate the dozens of OT prophecies Jesus fulfilled. They can be helpful resources.

Several of those OT-NT connections include:[14]

Thirty pieces of silver	Zech. 11:12	Matt. 26:14, 15
Betrayal of a friend	Ps. 55:12-14	Matt. 26:49, 50
Hit, spit upon	Isa. 50:6	Matt. 26:6, 7
Silent before accusers	Isa. 53:7	Matt. 27:12, 14
Wounded, beaten	Isa. 53:5	Matt. 27:26, 29
Hands and feet pierced	Ps. 22:16	Luke 23:33
Crucified with thieves	Isa. 53:12	Mark 15:27, 28
Forsaken cry	Ps. 22:1	Matt. 27:46
Given gall and vinegar	Ps. 69:21	John 19:28, 29
Bones not broken	Ps. 34:20	John 19:33, 36
Buried in a rich man's tomb	Isa. 53:9	Matt. 27:57-60

Second, the OT passage of Isaiah 53 is central to Judaism. This passage is one of the servant passages of Isaiah. Consider Isaiah's depiction of the "servant" of God as despised, rejected, sorrowful, and full of grief (v. 3). Jesus is described throughout the Gospels in the same language.

Isaiah likewise describes the Messiah's redemptive ministry as a substitutionary one: being buried in a tomb other than his own and dying an unimaginably gruesome death. All of these prophetic statements accurately predicted what actually happened to Jesus at the time of His crucifixion. Careful study and presentation of the connections between the suffering servant of Isaiah 53 and Jesus can be powerful for the Jewish seeker after truth.

The question, then, for the adherent to Judaism is: What will you do with Jesus? As C. S. Lewis said, He is either a liar, a lunatic, or the Lord. The New Testament builds the case for Jesus as the crucified Messiah prophesied in the Old Testament. Believing this central truth is not only a rational act based on reasonable evidence, but it is also the work of the Holy Spirit of God. Our task, whether we are speaking with a Jew, a Shinto, Buddhist, or Hindu, is to faithfully declare the truth. The response of the hearer is God's business.

FOR FURTHER DISCUSSION

1. What is your reaction to the controversial statement: "God Almighty doesn't hear the prayer of a Jew?" What lessons can Christians learn from the history of the relationship between Jews and Christians?

2. Which Jewish historical figure do you most admire? Why? In what ways was he important to both the Jewish and the Christian faith?

3. What spiritual lessons can we learn by examining the fall of Israel to Assyria in 722 B.C. and the fall of Judah to Babylonia in 586 B.C.?

4. Identify the distinctives of each of the sects of Judaism listed below. In what ways does this knowledge deepen your understanding of Matthew 22:15-40 and other passages like it?
   - Sadducees
   - Pharisees
   - Essenes

5. How might you use one or more of the Jewish customs and festivals as bridges to share the light of the gospel with Jews?

6. How would your approach to witnessing differ, depending on whether a Jew is Orthodox, Conservative, or Reform?

7. Summarize the various beliefs of Jewish groups about Messiah. Write a prayer asking God to open the eyes of Jews to accept Jesus as the Messiah.

8

Islam

THE MORNING OF September 11, 2001, forever changed the United States and the world. Muslim terrorists targeted a vital center of America's economic power (the World Trade Center), its military power (the Pentagon), and, although the plane crashed, presumably its political power (the White House or the Capitol). The United States is still dealing with the ramifications of that horrific event. Americans remain perplexed about the faith of Islam. How could a religion like Islam motivate young men to commandeer airplanes and fly them into buildings? How could a worldview like this produce such fanaticism? Is such fanaticism typical or an exception? Our world is complex, and its worldviews are complex, but there is probably no worldview currently more important than Islam.

As a term, "Islam" means suffering (for Allah, or God) and "Muslim" is one who suffers (for Allah, or God). Islam is a religion of remarkable discipline and rigor. It promotes a works-righteousness view of salvation that instructs the worshiper on how to merit the favor of Allah. How did this worldview develop?

ISLAM: ITS HISTORY

The founding and early history of Islam revolves around the prophet Muhammad (A.D. 570-632). Muhammad was born about 570. Because he lost his father near the time of his birth and because his mother died when he was six, Muhammad was cared for briefly by his grandfather and later by his uncle, Abu Talib. Abu Talib was a merchant; so Muhammad traveled extensively with him in the thriving caravan network that wound through Arabia, Syria, then into India and northern Africa. No doubt it was these journeys that first exposed Muhammad to Christianity and Judaism. Although none of these contacts were with orthodox representatives of either faith, a deepening conviction about the truth of monotheism resulted.

According to Muslim tradition, the year 610 changed Muhammad and consequently the world. On the seventeenth night of the month of Ramadan, Muhammad was in solitary meditation in a cave at the foot of Mount Hira, near the city of Mecca, when he suddenly saw a vision. The angel Gabriel commanded him to "recite." Not understanding what he was to recite, Muhammad heard Gabriel exclaim that he was the prophet of God (Allah). Muhammad's newfound monotheism was controversial among the polytheistic tribes of Mecca. Resistance from Mecca intensified, and his life was in danger.

According to Muslim tradition, Allah confirmed Muhammad's prophethood in 620, miraculously bringing him at night to Jerusalem. There he conversed with Jesus, Moses, and Abraham, and there he and Gabriel were taken by a ladder to the seventh heaven. (Muslims believe that the Dome of the Rock is built on the site of this ascension). Still his monotheistic message was rejected by his people.

Muhammad continued to condemn the paganism of the polytheistic Arabian tribes. In Mecca there was a massive stone shrine called the Ka'bah, which attracted pilgrims from all over Arabia. Fifty feet high and nearly forty feet square, it housed one idol for each day of the year. Some said it had been built by Adam and Eve after their expulsion from the Garden of Eden. Others claimed that Abraham and Ishmael had built it. Arabian pilgrims came to kiss or touch the smooth black stone that glistened in the southeastern corner of the city.

So severe was Muhammad's persecution that he took his wife and small group of followers and fled to Medina, about 250 miles north of Mecca. For the Muslim this momentous event, called the "Hijra," is year 1 in the Muslim calendar. While in Medina, Muhammad found acceptance and began to build his army of Islam. He had become a military leader!

Eight years after the Hijra, Muhammad and his army of 10,000 reentered Mecca in triumph. Thronged by his followers, the sixty-two-year-old commander led a glorious pilgrimage to the Ka'bah, now the focal point of Islamic worship. There in 632, he announced the perfection of a new religion—the worship of Allah. Before he died, Muhammad established complete domination over the Arabian peninsula.[1]

What was Muhammad's relationship with the early Christians and the Jews? He was not really familiar with Christianity, nor the Bible. The Qur'an, the 114 chapters of the archangel Gabriel's revelations to Muhammad, refutes Christian claims that Jesus died on the cross, that He was God's Son, and that God is triune. Likewise, the Qur'an alludes to other beliefs that are demonstrably false—that Mary was a sister of Aaron and Moses and that she was part of the Trinity. So Muhammad denied Jesus' deity, His atoning death on the cross, and the Trinitarian nature of God.[2]

Despite such error and misunderstanding of Christianity, Muhammad vigorously taught that he and his teachings were heirs to both Judaism and Christianity—those he called "peoples of the book." For that reason, Muhammad decreed that Christians and Jews were to receive protection under Muslim rule. He extended personal hospitality to Christians, but less to Jews. In fact, as Dr. Pat Cate demonstrates, when one evaluates the chapters of the Qur'an chronologically, a clear progression exists confirming hostility toward Jews and Christians.[3] During his early years in Mecca, Muhammad confirmed his basic allegiance with Jews and Christians. However, after the flight to Medina, he turned radically against them and developed his teachings about *jihad* (to be discussed later).

After Muhammad's death, Islam spread rapidly. In fact, in only a hundred years (632-732) it swept across the rest of Arabia, Palestine, all of northern Africa, and into Spain, only to be stopped in France. Why did it spread so quickly? The military vacuum left by the collapse of western Rome and the *jihad*, or holy war, proclaimed by the Qur'an help to explain the swift conquest. Huge territories, once dominated by Christianity, were lost, many of which have never been recovered to this day.

Muhammad had designated no successor to take up his cause. His followers had to decide the manner of the succession—was it to be based on heredity or on loyalty to Muhammad? The successors could not come to an agreement, which caused a fatal division in Islam that has never healed. According to the Sunni sect (the Traditionalists), the Medinans selected an aging member from Muhammad's tribe, Abu Bakr, Muhammad's father-in-law. But, according to the Shiah sect (partisans of Ali), the prophet's cousin and son-in-law was the designated successor—Ali ibn Abi Talib. For the sake of unity, Ali ultimately deferred to Abu Bakr, but Islam today remains divided between the Sunnis and the Shiites.

The remaining history of Islam can be summarized in the following manner:

• After the first four caliphates (rulers/followers of Muhammad), the Umayyad tribe gained political control of Islam and formed a dynasty that lasted from 661-750. It was the Umayyads that spread Islam across northern Africa and into Spain. Islam remained militant and militaristic during this period.

• The next dynasty, the Abbasids, followed after a successful revolt against the Umayyads. This dynasty lasted from 750 to 1055 and was characterized by peace, not war. Its political center was Baghdad, and the Abbasid courts were filled with luxury and wealth that resulted from prolific trade policies. The Abbasid dynasty is considered the high water mark of Islamic culture.

• In the 1050s, the Seljuk Turks gained control of Islam. Coming from central Asia, the Turks were brutal and aggressive and destroyed the peaceful court of the Abbasids. They denied Christians access to the Holy Land, which sparked the Crusades (1096-1200s), an attempt by Christian Europe to drive the Muslims out.

• The Ottoman Turks succeeded their cousins, the Seljuk Turks, and conquered the eastern empire centered in Istanbul (1454) and invaded Europe. Much of central and southern Europe fell under Muslim control as a result.

• The modern period of Islamic history (much of the twentieth century) is characterized by nationalism mixing with Islam in the emergence of modern Islamic nation states such as Egypt, Iran, Turkey, Saudi Arabia, Kuwait, and Iraq. Although Islam continues to expand as a faith, it is wrapped up in the larger geopolitical issues of global trade in oil, terrorism, political alliances, and the larger Israeli-Palestinian conflict. As a faith, Islam is the fastest growing world religion; as a political/economic force in an age of terrorism, it is at the center of today's world events.

ISLAM AS A WORLDVIEW: ITS THEOLOGY AND ITS ETHICS

God: The Muslim concept of God is summed up in the name "Allah." A critical point for Islamic doctrine is the stress on Allah's unity of being. This dominates the Muslim's thinking about God and is expressed in the phrase, "There is no God but Allah." He is absolutely unique and inconceivable. An Islamic proverb says, "Whatever your mind may think of, God is not that!" A constant phrase repeated in Muslim prayers is "Allah akbar" (God is great). God is far greater than any thought humans can have of him. Allah is so great that he can do what he likes, even break his own laws.

In Islam, Allah has decreed all that will occur. He is the creator of all that is in heaven and on earth. His knowledge is perfect; his will is beyond challenge; and his power is irresistible. All of these attributes—omniscience, sovereignty, and omnipotence—are evident in his creation. Many pious Muslims carry a rosary that has ninety-nine beads, each one representing one of Allah's names. The one-hundredth name is unknown to humans; according to Muslim legend, only the camel knows it.

Allah's might and majesty are tempered with justice. He rewards and punishes; yet he is merciful, a guardian of his servants, defender of the orphan, guide of the wrongdoer, liberator from pain, friend of the poor, and ready-to-forgive master.[4]

Allah resides in the seventh heaven, far removed from his creation. He is unknowable, but he has chosen to make himself known through the holy books and through his prophets. The books include the Old and New Testaments, and the prophets include the prophets of the Old Testament and Jesus.

Angels and Evil Spirits: Allah is surrounded by angels—pure, sexless beings who worship and adore him. Angels also serve as messengers from Allah to his people and fight for the true Muslim believers. Some of them are known as the good "jinn," as the guardian angels of man, who not only guard humans but also keep records for the day of judgment. Other angels guard hell to insure that all who are condemned to go there, stay there.

The fear of evil spirits plays a prominent role in the lives of Muslims. They believe that the entire universe is inhabited by both good and bad jinn. Chief among the evil jinn is the devil or Satan. Once an angel, Allah expelled him from heaven for refusing to bow to Adam at Allah's command. Most Muslims believe in Satan and continually ask Allah for protection from him.

The Holy Books: Muslims maintain that Allah handed down 104 books, and of these, only four are most important. They believe that the Law was given to Moses; that the Psalms were given to David; that the Gospels were given to Jesus, and that the Qur'an was given to Muhammad. Muhammad made no claim that his teaching invalidated the Jewish and Christian Scriptures; rather he instructed both

Christians and Jews to follow their respective teachings[5] and commanded Muslims to believe in and obey the Law and the Psalms.[6] He taught that the Gospels were sent to confirm and safeguard the Law, which served as guidance and light to those who fear Allah.[7] The Qur'an safeguards both the Law and the Gospels.[8]

The Prophets: Muslims believe that Allah sent 124,000 prophets and apostles, but that the three greatest prophets were Moses, Jesus, and Muhammad. Muhammad, the Qur'an teaches, is the last and the greatest prophet, for he proclaimed Allah's final revelation. The heart of his message was one of morality, a call to righteousness. That meant abandoning polytheism and paganism and submitting totally to the will of Allah. His message, however, also involved community. Islam would create a new fellowship based on loyalty to Allah and to one another. The old loyalties to clan, tribe, nation, and state would be set aside for loyalty to Allah. For that reason, even today, Muslims of all clans, tribes, and nations gather in Mecca. Islam refuses to separate church and state, and Islamic judges always respect the consensus of the community.[9]

The Day of Judgment: The inevitability of divine judgment permeates the Qur'an. In Sura 2, it is described as the Day of Gathering, when there will be a group in Paradise and one in the Fire. It teaches that Allah will take a scale and weigh the good and evil deeds of each person. If the good outweighs the bad—paradise; otherwise hell. But for Muslims, Allah is great and merciful, and Muhammad intercedes for them. The result is that Allah's decision on judgment is more related to his will than to his justice. The Qur'an offers little assurance on this matter of eternity.

The Pillars of Islamic Practice: Submission and obedience constitute the core of Islam. By good deeds, the Muslim expresses his commitment to Allah. The moral and ritual obligations of Muslims are summed up in the five pillars of Islam:

• *Pillar 1: The Witness.* To make the profession, "There is no God but Allah, and Muhammad is his prophet," is to become a Muslim. In uttering the first part, one submits to Allah; by uttering the second, one becomes an adherent of Islam. This profession is not to be taken lightly. It begins with an affirmation of Allah and his oneness. It continues with the means by which Allah reveals himself to humanity—through Muhammad.

• *Pillar 2: The Ritual Prayers.* Every devout Muslim performs the ritual prayers at least five times a day. There are the prayers of the morning, at midday, midway between midday and sunset, at sunset, and one hour after sunset. Ritual prayers mainly are praises to Allah and are always recited in Arabic.

In most Muslim countries, a spiritual leader, called a "muezzin," mounts the balcony of the minarets that dot Muslim city skylines and calls Muslims to prayer. The prayer is recited in any location a Muslim finds himself, although urban Muslims usually gather in the mosques. All face the direction of Mecca when they pray—to remind them of the birthplace of their faith.

• *Pillar 3: The Paying of Alms.* Paying alms is giving back to Allah a portion of his bounty in order to avoid suffering in the next life and as a purification of what one retains materially. It is not voluntary, but is an obligation to gain favor with Allah.

• *Pillar 4: The Fast of Ramadan.* The fast of Ramadan is an obligatory duty for all Muslims (except the sick, pregnant women, travelers under certain conditions, and soldiers in combat). Because Muslims follow the lunar calendar, Ramadan lasts thirty days, and in each successive year it occurs about nine days earlier than the previous year. Each day the fast begins from the moment one awakes, and it lasts until sunset. The night is spent eating and drinking. During the day of the fast, the Qur'an prohibits eating, drinking, smoking, swallowing saliva, and sex. The fast is a debt owed to Allah, and it atones for sin, helps control passions, and merits favor with Allah.

• *Pillar 5: The Pilgrimage to Mecca.* This obligation to Allah is to be performed at least once during a Muslim's life. The pilgrimage is filled with ritualistic observances such as stopping at the well where Gabriel heard Hannah's plea for water, the place where Satan is believed to have been stoned, and kissing the sacred black stone of the Ka'bah.[10]

A Word About Jihad: The term *jihad* literally means "struggle" or "exertion." In the religious context it always involves a struggle against evil. That struggle can involve one of the heart, where the Muslim fights the evil of his nature, but it can also be a "jihad of the mouth," where the Muslim struggles against those who oppose Islam. The most controversial form of jihad is the "jihad of the sword."

Throughout the Qur'an there are calls to physical combat on behalf of Islam. In fact, this doctrine developed over time in Muhammad's teaching. In the Qur'an chapters that focus on his time in Mecca and even early Medina, the militancy of jihad is absent. However, as the opposition to Islam mounted, so did Muhammad's teaching that jihad is military force in the name of Allah. As the doctrine developed,

Muhammad taught that those who sacrificed their lives in the battle for Allah were guaranteed admission to the highest level of heaven. Jihad became a violent military means of spreading the faith, and Allah was glorified through it. Historically, jihad became the heart of Islam's expansion. Today Islamic terrorists are trying to resurrect that militant, aggressive form of jihad.[11]

At the beginning of this chapter, I posed the question as to whether the fanaticism seen on September 11, 2001, is typical of Islam. Within the entire spectrum of Islam, such fanaticism is not typical (e.g., Egypt, Kuwait, Jordan, Saudi Arabia, Turkey, etc.). The vast majority of Muslims are not committed to fanatical jihad where killing civilians in terrorist attacks is a holy cause. However, to the followers of Osama bin Laden, al Qaeda, the Palestinian terrorists of Hamas, Hezbollah, and Islamic Jihad, fanatical jihad is becoming the norm. Many of these terrorists were radicalized in the war against the Soviet Union in Afghanistan during the 1980s. They defeated a superpower there, and now they believe they can do so against the United States, which they regard as corrupt, decadent, and ultimately weak. Such groups believe they can destroy Israel and the United States. Although small, such groups can wreak devastation, fear, and destruction on their enemies. Such fanaticism will not be easily defeated.

BUILDING BRIDGES TO THE MUSLIM

Charles R. Marsh, a pioneer missionary in Algeria, offers several guidelines for communicating the gospel to Muslims. Each is an effective bridge to Islam:

Bridge #1

Avoid condemning Islam or speaking in a derogatory manner about Muhammad. Instead of criticizing Islam outright, one must seek to understand it. This involves being a good listener. When speaking with a Muslim, it is generally wise to allow the Muslim to speak first. Courtesy, respect, and honor are important in Islamic culture.

Bridge #2

Remember that a Muslim is a believer in god. Islam is monotheistic, and Allah shares many of the same attributes as the true God of the Bible. This is the common ground upon which a relationship can be built.

Bridge #3

In the heart of every Muslim is the fear of Allah. The Qur'an teaches that every Muslim will someday stand before him. Most Muslims have anxiety that they are not doing enough to merit Allah's favor. The Christian must be able to communicate the critical concept of grace. For Christians, the fear of God is not based on terror; it is reverence and awe for the one with whom we have a personal relationship. This point is crucial for Muslims because they have no concept of a personal relationship with the living God.

Bridge #4

Most Muslims have a certain sense of sin, rooted largely in their failure to attain Allah's high standards. Islam gives no assurance of pardon for sin. Here is where the Christian message takes hold, for Jesus provided that assurance on Calvary's cross.

Bridge #5

Make use of the truth that Muslims know to lead them to the whole truth about God's Word. Muslims already know that God is light and that in Him there is no darkness at all. They know Jesus is the son of Mary and that one of His titles is the Word of God. They know that Jesus will soon return to reign. They know that humans must be pure to approach God. Once a relationship is established, the Word of God can be used to corroborate what Islam teaches and provide further instruction regarding the true nature of Christianity.

Bridge #6

Because the Qur'an rejects God as Trinitarian, it is difficult for Muslims to grasp the deity of Jesus. For that reason, once a relationship of trust is established, it is imperative to focus on the deity of Jesus, perhaps using such verses as Matthew 3:16,17; 17:5; 28:19; John 10:30; 14:6; 8:58; Romans 8:26-27; 1 Peter 1:2.

Muslims also stumble over Jesus as the Son of God because often they teach that God cohabited with Mary to produce Jesus. What we as Christians must do is demonstrate that Jesus' sonship describes His relationship to the other members of the Godhead; sonship is not proof that He had a point of origin or beginning. Jesus is the manifestation of the unseen God (see Heb. 1:1-3 and Col. 1:15-20).[12]

Islam is one of the most difficult religions to penetrate with the gospel. For that reason, the establishment of a relationship with Muslims is imperative. Once trust and confidence are present, the Holy Spirit will have the freedom to move in the hearts of Muslims through us. We must know Islam, and we must be willing to spend time with those who follow it.

FOR FURTHER DISCUSSION

1. What insights do the definitions for "Islam" and "Muslim" give you into the Islamic faith?
2. What was impressive or not so impressive to you about Muhammad and his founding of Islam?
3. After a review of Islam's history, what new perspectives have you gained about this religion and its wide influence? What do you predict will be the influence of Islam in the future?
4. What inconsistencies do you see with the Muslim affirmation of both the Gospels and the Qur'an? How might this be used as a bridge to Muslims?
5. Compare and contrast the five pillars of Islamic practice with Christian disciplines. In what ways are the motivations for the disciplines different?
6. How would your faith be affected if you accepted the Muslim belief that God was unpredictable and unknowable in a personal way?
7. In what practical, respectful ways could you demonstrate your personal relationship with God to a Muslim friend? Develop friendships with Muslims and begin to build your bridges to their lives.

9

The New Age Movement

PERHAPS NO OTHER modern figure personifies the New Age worldview better than Shirley MacLaine, the Hollywood actress. In 1987, based on her book *Out on a Limb*, her life story was told on an ABC miniseries. That TV series legitimized the New Age worldview and presented it in a popular format so that millions could view a woman transformed by New Age teachings. Listen to Shirley MacLaine describe her worldview:

> Regardless of how I looked at the riddle of life, it always came down to one thing: personal identity, personal reality. Having complete dominion and understanding of myself was the answer to harmony, balance, and peace. . . .
>
> If I created my own reality, then—on some level and dimension I didn't understand—I had created everything I saw, heard, touched, smelled, tasted; everything I loved, hated, revered, abhorred; everything I responded to or that responded to me. Then I created everything I knew. I was therefore responsible for all there was in my reality. . . . I was my own universe. Did that mean I had created God and I had created life and death? . . .
>
> Was this what was meant by the statement I AM THAT I AM?[1]

In MacLaine's comments we see major themes associated with the New Age worldview: Self defines reality; self is all that really matters; self is in effect God; self is the center of everything. At first glance, this worldview seems utterly bizarre; yet today it appeals to millions of people in Western civilization.

The New Age Movement (NAM) is virtually impossible to define. It has no central leader and no major texts that specify its cardinal tenets. There is no geographical center to the movement and there is no consensus of theology or agenda. It is an amorphous movement that perplexes many and yet energizes so many more. Can we determine its history and unravel its powerful appeal?

THE HISTORY OF THE NEW AGE MOVEMENT

Although New Age thinking is rooted deeply in ideas associated with Eastern pantheism, occult groups of the nineteenth century, and other mystical movements, the 1960s appear to be the decisive decade for the formation of the NAM. First, the 1960s witnessed the first major change in immigration laws, where laws that excluded people coming from the East were repealed and large numbers of Asians poured into America, including countless teachers of Eastern religions such as Buddhism and Hinduism. Gradually those ideas mixed with Western thought to produce the hybrid called the New Age. Furthermore, popular music groups, especially the Beatles, sought out Eastern gurus as they pursued truth and life's purpose. Many of these Eastern gurus came to America and gathered large numbers of followers.[2]

New Age thinking comes essentially out of a fusion of Eastern and Western belief systems. It combines the Western naturalist commitment to the Darwinian hypothesis, which sees natural selection as the key to explaining all forms of life, and Eastern thought, which rejects reason as the sole means to understanding the world. There is a spiritual realm beyond the physical, but that realm is discernible only through means that raise human consciousness. As that level of consciousness is reached, the NAM teaches, the next stage of human evolution will be upon us. This strange fusion of ideas produces the optimistic, energized dynamic of the New Age.[3]

Second, in 1968 Carlos Castaneda published the first of four novels called *The Teaching of Don Juan: The Yagui Way of Knowledge,* a book that stressed South American sorcery as the key to a "New Consciousness." This concept, New Consciousness, entered the vocabulary of the West as a popular phrase and goal for life. Its impact on the college community was especially decisive.

Third, the discipline of psychology was transformed into a hotbed of New Age thinking. Psychologists such as Abraham Maslow, Carl Rogers, and Rollo May refocused much of popular psychology from dealing with pathology to helping people develop through a more transcendental and humanistic approach. For example, Maslow talked much about "self-actualization" as the goal of popular psychological thinking and counseling. Maslow's self-actualized human was a truly satisfied, fulfilled human, essentially "full of self." This new approach to psychology "was a psychology that glorified self. It pronounced people's impulses essentially good, affirmed the unfathomable depths of human potential, and held out personal growth as an individual's highest goal."[4] As Douglas Groothius comments, "Human experience is thus the center and source of meaning and is valuable apart from any dependence on or subservience to a higher power."[5]

Fourth, the growing influence of Eastern thinking and popular psychology's emphasis on the human potential combined to transform almost all disciplines of human knowledge and professional practice. James Sire details the impact of this synthesis of Eastern thought and human potential psychology:

• Within the fields of psychology and psychiatry, there was a new openness to using drugs to determine the purpose and meaning of life. Some researchers in these fields used LSD and other mind-altering drugs to foster "cosmic unity" and "consciousness." In addition, some psychologists and psychiatrists began to study biofeedback of alpha and beta waves as a means to producing altered states of consciousness.

• In the fields of sociology and cultural history, the NAM was legitimized through the works of Theodore Rozak, George Leonard, and William Irwin Thompson. Each of these respectable scholars took NAM ideas and worked them into their disciplines, thereby gaining increased acceptability for the NAM.

• In anthropology, the works of Carlos Castaneda (previously mentioned) have been decisive in introducing thousands of college students to the teaching of the NAM. Castaneda spent years studying sorcery and the use of psychedelic drugs to alter consciousness among members of Latin American Indian culture. His works are now standard NAM books.

• Remarkably, even in the sciences NAM thinking is prevalent. There are now popular NAM interpretations of physics and biology in the works of Gary Zukav and Lewis Thomas.

• In the fields of popularized medicine and health there is an abundance of evidence that NAM is defining the future of these fields. Acupuncture, Rolfing, psychic healing, kinesiology, and therapeutic touch are only a few of the NAM practices mainstreamed in the West today.

• In politics, the most important area of influence has been in the environmental arena. Groups that are politically active and lobby for NAM goals are the Sierra Club and the Green Party in Germany. Such organizations are pervasive and extraordinarily powerful in Western Europe, where they actually define much of the political agenda.

• In science fiction, one sees significant NAM influence. Arthur Clarke's book and Stanley Kubrick's movie *2001* (1968) conclude with the dawning of a New Age child—"the Star-Child." Robert A. Heinlein's *Stranger in a Strange Land* (1961) was for years an underground classic in the NAM. The works of Philip K. Dick are currently the most important vehicle for NAM thought in this genre of writing.

• In Hollywood movies we see the most powerful communication of NAM ideas. Arguably, the most significant example is the highly popular and ongoing Star Wars series by George Lucas. The Force is the divine power guiding the world, and the goal of each human is to be in touch with the good side of the Force. Yoda is the NAM guru of the original trilogy of the Star Wars series.

• In athletics, sports, and personal exercise programs, NAM practices and ideas are prominent. Kung fu, judo, karate, and aikido are martial arts programs rooted in Eastern techniques that may involve altered states of consciousness. Professional baseball, basketball, and football players are increasingly involved in meditative programs like yoga that relax them and enhance their powers of concentration.[6]

The influence of the NAM is extensive, touching nearly every facet of our culture. NAM ideas enable the modern person to keep all of the Western naturalistic ideas associated with Darwin and modernity and yet add a spiritually satisfying dimension to life. This curious mix of East and West in the NAM is no longer a fad; it is a part of our world— it is mainstreamed. What was once the "lunatic fringe" is now an acceptable worldview option. What is its theology, and how does that theology impact ethics?

THE NEW AGE: ITS THEOLOGY AND ITS ETHICS

God: At the heart of NAM theology is pantheism, which holds that everything and everyone is God. God is an impersonal, undifferentiated force or principle, not separate nor distinct from the physical world. Humans must raise their consciousness to understand that they are God. This point manifests the governing principle of the NAM, namely that self is the prime reality. Self defines and names reality, which we see in the comments by Shirley MacLaine that opened this chapter. She questions whether she "had created God" and "had created life and death."[7]

How does the NAM raise consciousness so that humans can realize that they are indeed God? A myriad of "doors" to open this level of consciousness are suggested by the NAM. Among them are certain drugs, meditation, trances, biofeedback, ritualized dance, certain kinds of music, channeling (a form of séance), using crystals, etc. Each of these "doors" enables human beings to come to terms with the truth that they are indeed "God" and that they know no dimensions of any kind. Listen to Shirley MacLaine: "I was learning to recognize the invisible dimension where there are no measurements possible. In fact, it is the dimension of no-height, no-width, no-breadth, and no-mass, and as a matter of further fact, no-time. It is the dimension of the spirit."[8]

James Sire explains further: "When the self perceives itself to be at one with the cosmos, it is at one with it. Self-realization, then, is the realization that self and the cosmos are not only of a piece but are the same piece."[9] This statement defines the ultimate goal of the NAM, which is summarized as "cosmic consciousness."

Jesus: For the NAM, Jesus is not the one true God. He is not the Savior, but a spiritual model, a guru, and as some state, "an ascended master." He was a New Ager who achieved "cosmic consciousness" and "rose" into a higher spiritual realm of consciousness. That is the nature of his "resurrection." For the NAM, to speak of Jesus as God is not difficult, but to speak of Him as the unique, one true God, whose death and resurrection were substitutionary for human sin, is ludicrous. He is a spiritual guru, not the Savior.

Sin: The concept of sin as the Bible defines it is a foreign concept to the NAM. They see sin as the absence of enlightenment, of cosmic consciousness. There is no need for an atonement for human sin; rather, there is the need for proper methods to raise that consciousness.

Most NAM members believe in reincarnation. However, unlike Hinduism, which regards reincarnation as a curse and a horrific cycle that must be broken, the NAM regards reincarnation as a more positive part of the cosmic cycle of evolution, where the human race achieves the higher stage of cosmic consciousness. Once that realization occurs, ultimate consciousness is attained, and reincarnation ends. There will then be mass enlightenment and greater human unity. As Gruss elaborates, "This unity will transcend the individual and social self-centeredness that has created the present crises in the environment, world hunger, international relations, racism, etc."[10] Humans will have attained the "Age of Aquarius."

Ethics—Good and Evil: As epitomized in the Star Wars trilogies of movies, the NAM sees both good and evil as part of the Force. The NAM does not make clear distinctions between good and evil, right and wrong. Further, what makes it more difficult is that the self for the NAM is really sovereign, the center of all things. Self creates its own reality. The result is that self defines good and evil, with the end being no ethical absolutes. For example, in Shirley MacLaine's first NAM book, *Out on a Limb,* and the subsequent ABC television program, she justifies an adulterous affair with a member of the British Parliament by claiming that they were lovers in another life. So they run along the seashore of England screaming, "I am God. I am God."[11] With self defining reality, anything can ultimately be justified as acceptable. There are simply no ethical absolutes to guide human behavior. It is self living out its own conscious reality.

In conclusion, Douglas Groothuis analyzes the NAM as a "counterfeit religion." Several of its unifying ideas can be distilled into a basic worldview, which Groothuis summarizes in nine doctrines:

1. Evolutionary Optimism: A Counterfeit Kingdom. [Christians look to Christ's return for the kingdom.]
2. Monism: A Counterfeit Cosmos. [All is not one (monism). God created a world filled with diversity and plurality.]
3. Pantheism: A Counterfeit God and Humanity. [God is personal, and humans are not divine.]
4. Transformation of Consciousness: Counterfeit Conversion. [True conversion is not the realization of one's deity through one of the NAM "doors."]
5. Create Your Own Reality: Counterfeit Morality. [Biblical morality is grounded in the moral character of a personal God and His moral will revealed in Scripture.]
6. Unlimited Human Potential: Counterfeit Miracles. [Humans are limited by sin, depravity, and finiteness.]
7. Spirit Contact: Counterfeit Revelations. [Occult practices associated with the NAM open humans to contact with demonic powers, not the true God.]
8. Masters from Above: Counterfeit Angels. [Claims of UFO and extraterrestrial sightings validate NAM teachings about self and consciousness, all clearly contradicted by Scripture.]

9. Religious Syncretism: Counterfeit Religion. The NAM is a mixture of Eastern mysticism, occult practices, and Western humanism. [Both the Old and New Testaments condemn syncretism because it destroys the uniqueness of Jesus and the gospel (John 14:6 and Acts 4:12.)][12]

BUILDING BRIDGES TO THE NEW AGE MOVEMENT

In an "Open Letter to the New Agers," former New Age advocate Randall Baer invites members of the NAM to consider Jesus Christ:

> I testify to you, in love and compassion, that what I found when I accepted Jesus as my Lord and personal Savior opened my eyes to seeing truth in a totally different way, a much grander way than anything I ever knew in the New Age. What I have experienced as a Christian *far* surpasses even the most incredible, mind-blowing mystical experiences I had as a New Ager.[13]

Christians need to understand the complexities of the NAM but also be willing to reach out to NAM advocates.

Bridge #1

The most important place to start is to build relationships with NAM advocates. Members of the NAM are seeking something that thrills and awes, but many have also found that nothing really satisfies. Mystical experiences, rituals, and other fantastic elements of the New Age ultimately do not bring the satisfaction and fulfillment that all seek. Therefore, the authenticity and genuineness of the Christian life can speak volumes to a person embracing NAM. If they see the fruit of the Spirit (Gal. 5:22-23) and the Beatitudes of Jesus (Matt. 5:1-16) lived out, God's Spirit can use this supernatural life to attract them to genuine faith in Christ.

Bridge #2

Because the NAM stresses so heavily the sovereignty of self, it is imperative to press the point that self acting out its own desires and wants naturally results in the abandonment of all ethical standards and absolutes. If self is in the driver's seat in all areas and is satisfied, then who sets the boundaries for life? Who or what determines right and wrong? The result is moral and ethical anarchy, and no one who is intellectually honest can accept that. This remains one of the most vulnerable aspects of NAM thinking.[14]

Bridge #3

A third area to focus on with the NAM is the realm of the spirit world. For the person centered in the NAM, the world is filled with the supernatural, the spiritual, and the angelic. As Sire argues, "The New Age has reopened a door closed since Christianity drove out the demons from the woods, desacralized the natural world and generally took a dim view of excessive interest in the affairs of Satan's kingdom of fallen angels. Now they are back, knocking on university dorm-room doors, sneaking around psychology laboratories and chilling the spines of Ouija players."[15] As NAM advocates open themselves to this spirit world, there will be consequences, including demon possession, power, and occult activities. As Christians, we know that God is far more powerful than the spirit world, for He is its Creator. Deuteronomy 18:9-14 clearly prohibits any form of dabbling in the occult world, practices so central to the NAM. Jesus cast out numerous demons and offered freedom to millions. We must be ready to declare the truth about the occult world but also to offer the freedom that Jesus Christ brings from such enslavement. The fact is unmistakable: The NAM is a worldview deeply influenced by the occult.

Bridge #4

The NAM movement defines truth in a self-centered manner. Sire maintains that in the NAM "there is no critique of anyone's ideas or anyone's experience. Every system is equally valid; it must only pass the test of experience; and experience is private."[16] The end result is that in the NAM people can only know what they experience. But that rarely satisfies anyone. History has shown us that just experiencing all the facets of life, even those fantastic ones of the NAM, does not produce fulfillment or bring purpose. Jesus said that He had come that we might have life and have it more abundantly (John 10:10). As Christians, our task is both to live and to declare with our words that abundant life. If we have established a genuine relationship of trust and confidence with a member of the NAM, God can use our lives to point them to life's meaning and purpose, not in the mysticism of the NAM, but in Jesus Christ.

FOR FURTHER DISCUSSION

1. What is your reaction to Shirley MacLaine's New Age worldview? Which other worldviews studied so far in this text are similar?

2. The author suggests that the 1960s were critical to the popularization of New Age ideas. Explain some of the developments of the 1960s.

3. Where have you personally seen reflections of New Age ideas in the following areas?
   - psychology
   - anthropology
   - medicine
   - athletics
   - Hollywood movies

4. List a Scripture verse or passage that contradicts each of the New Age ideas about:
   - God
   - Jesus
   - sin
   - angels
   - good and evil

5. Which parts of New Age theology are reminiscent of Buddhist and Hindu views?

6. Write a letter to a New Age friend, incorporating several evangelistic bridges.

10

The Jehovah's Witness, Christian Science, and Mormon Worldviews

HISTORICALLY, THE United States of America has been a deeply religious nation, especially in its commitment to Protestant evangelicalism. In many ways this commitment to evangelicalism has meshed well with the political culture of America with its emphasis on liberty, personal responsibility, and individualism. This shared consensus has provided the basis for the nation's ethics and values for most of its history. Ironically, this freedom has also spawned major cults that today are growing in numbers and challenging this consensus and even the limits of what freedom of religion in America means.

This chapter seeks to summarize and analyze three of these cults—the Jehovah's Witnesses, Christian Science, and Mormonism. Obviously in a book this size, a comprehensive summary and analysis are not possible. What is possible are salient summaries that stress the history and then the similarities and distinctives of each cult. A discussion on how to reach each cult with the truth of the gospel will end this chapter.

First of all, the term "cult" needs defining. Theologian Anthony Hoekema offers perhaps the best set of distinctives:

1. An Extra-Scriptural Source of Authority;
2. The Denial of Justification by Faith Alone;
3. The Devaluation of Jesus Christ and His Uniqueness;
4. The Group as the Exclusive Community of the Saved.[1]

With these four distinctives in mind, we shall examine three major cults born in nineteenth-century America.

THE HISTORY OF THE JEHOVAH'S WITNESSES, CHRISTIAN SCIENCE, AND MORMON CULTS

Jehovah's Witnesses

The founder of this cult was Charles Taze Russell (1852-1916). Heavily influenced by Seventh Day Adventism in his early years, Russell broke with the Adventists and began publishing his own magazine, *Zion's Watchtower and Herald of Christ's Presence.* In 1884 he founded the Zion Watchtower Tract Society. A voluminous writer, Russell's most important work was a seven-volume series titled *Studies in the Scriptures,* published over the period from 1886 to 1904. Because he was a man of questionable character and ethics, Russell has been disowned by modern-day Jehovah's Witnesses.

Russell was succeeded in 1917 by Joseph Franklin Rutherford. Rutherford gained absolute control over the Watchtower Society, and in 1931, following Isaiah 43:10, he renamed the movement Jehovah's Witnesses. He also denounced all organized religions and fostered a tone of hostility toward Christianity. Rutherford built on the teachings of Russell and became an even more prolific writer.

Nathan Homer Knorr followed Rutherford, and under his leadership the Jehovah's Witnesses stressed intense training for their disciples. The image of the movement changed. It became more respectable and highly organized. The movement's training of its layman and its leaders took place in what are known today as Kingdom Halls.

Why are Jehovah's Witnesses so aggressive and energetic? Because of their eschatology (doctrine of the end times). As Boa demonstrates, Witnesses teach that Christ's second coming has already occurred. It involved three stages: in 1874, Christ came to the "upper air" and later caught up the apostles and dead members of the 144,000, who will be immortal; in 1914 Christ ended the times of the Gentiles and began to reign; in 1918 He came to the spiritual temple and began the judgment of the nations. Witnesses now eagerly await the imminent battle of Armageddon in which Jesus will lead Jehovah's forces to defeat evil. Only faithful Witnesses will escape death in this battle,[2] and only those who earn their place among the Witnesses through their door-to-door work are the "saved."

In the Witnesses door-to-door ministry, their most effective tools are their publications—*The Watchtower* and *Awake!*, the two predominant ones. Included in *The Watchtower* are doctrinal treatises and historical reviews of how the Witness movement developed. The other major publication of the Society is *The New World Translation of the Holy Scriptures*, completed in 1960. Hoekema writes of this "translation" that it "is by no means an objective rendering of the sacred text into modern English, but is a biased translation in which many of the peculiar teachings of the Watchtower Society are smuggled into the text of the Bible itself."[3] Witnesses are aggressive and passionate in their use of this translation.

Christian Science

The founder of Christian Science was Mary Baker Eddy. Born in 1821, Eddy was raised by strict Congregationalist parents, and her youth was characterized by various illnesses and spinal problems. Her first husband, George Washington Glover, died of yellow fever, which along with the birth of her son a few months later, affected her emotionally and mentally. These difficulties continued into her second marriage to Daniel M. Patterson, which later ended in divorce.

During her marriage to Patterson, she traveled to Portland, Maine, where she was healed of her spinal problems by "Dr." P. P. Quimby, who had developed a system of mental healing that he called "The Science of Health" or "Christian Science." Seemingly cured by his techniques, Mary Baker Glover Patterson became an ardent disciple of his teaching and incorporated much of his work into her book *Science and Health* (1875). In later years, she denied her dependence on Quimby, but in reality she took his ideas and assimilated them into her religious convictions.

On February 1, 1866, she fell on an icy sidewalk and was, she claims, given only three days to live. On the third day, she read Matthew 9:2, after which she was miraculously healed. This she dates as the beginning of her discovery of Christian Science. Although this story remains highly suspect, it marks the beginning of this cult.

In 1877 she married Asa Eddy and became Mary Baker Glover Patterson Eddy. The rest of her life she devoted to teaching the principles of Christian Science, which she systematized in her text *Science and Health*. She formed the official organization called The Christian Scientists, which was incorporated in 1879 as Church of Christ, Scientist, with the mother church located in Boston.

The Christian Science movement grew significantly over the next decades, marking more than 200,000 members by 1900. Mary Baker

Eddy was the undisputed authority over the church, even claiming to be Christ's successor. She died in 1910 at the age of eighty-nine, leaving an estate valued at $3 million.[4]

As Boa makes clear, Mary Baker Eddy was not well educated, and "she knew nothing about philosophy, logic, theology, Hebrew, Greek, or biblical history."[5] The earliest editions of her work are filled with grammatical errors, later corrected. Her work is also saturated with repetition, jargon, and rambling sentences. "The material is disjointed and far removed from any logical sequence."[6]

To promote its worldview, the Christian Science movement has published the rather prestigious *Christian Science Monitor* newspaper. But changes and increased competition in the newspaper industry have made the newspaper unprofitable. The Christian Science leadership also experimented with operating a cable news channel, a magazine, and a Boston radio station.[7] Today the church publishes the following:

• *Christian Science Quarterly,* weekly Bible lessons that combine the Bible and the works of Eddy in *Science and Health* into a weekly study format

• *The Christian Science Journal,* which offers instructive articles and "verified" reports of Christian healing and the work of the "divine Principle"

• *Christian Science Sentinel*, which comments on world events and trends and relates them to Christian Science principles

• *The Christian Science Monitor*, a scaled-down newspaper published internationally. [For a review of these publications see the church Web site at www.tfccs.com]

Today the Christian Science movement continues to maintain Reading Rooms in major cities across the nation. Each Room is filled with the works of Mrs. Eddy and other related literature. Church membership has plummeted in the last few decades, with only about 2,400 churches presently in the movement.

Mormonism

Of the three cults discussed in this chapter, Mormonism is by far the largest and fastest growing, with as many as ten million adherents worldwide. Its founder, Joseph Smith, Jr., was born December 23, 1805, in Sharon, Vermont. From an early age, Joseph was greatly influenced by his father, who curiously spent a great deal of time searching for buried treasure using unorthodox and often occult methods. Joseph Smith's life changed in 1820 when he supposedly received a vision from God the Father and the Son, who told him that all other religions were an abomination, but that he was the prophet to bring restoration.

In 1823 another vision from the angel Moroni further solidified Smith's charge from God. The angel informed him that he would uncover a number of golden plates that needed translating. Smith discovered these plates, inscribed with what he called "reformed Egyptian hieroglyphics," outside Palmyra, New York. He was able to translate them with a huge pair of spectacles that he called the "Urim and Thummim." According to his story, between 1827 and 1829, he "translated" the plates, and in 1830 published *The Book of Mormon.* The plates were purportedly taken to heaven by Moroni.

In 1829, Smith founded the Church of Jesus Christ of Latter-Day Saints. After a few relocations, Smith finally brought his religious headquarters to Illinois where Mormons built the city of Nauvoo and Smith instituted the practice of polygamy. When Smith and his brother Hyrum tried to destroy a local newspaper office because of its stand against the Mormons, they were arrested and jailed in Carthage, Illinois. Tragically, an angry mob stormed the prison, and on June 27, 1844, shot and killed the two brothers, making them martyrs. The leadership mantle passed to Brigham Young, the First President and prophet of the church.

Under Young's leadership, the Mormons relocated to Salt Lake City in July 1847. There they settled and built their unique brand of religion. In the face of U.S. governmental regulations, Mormon leaders eventually abolished polygamy as a doctrine.

Today the Mormons are a highly structured and organized religion. Led by a First President, a Council of Twelve Apostles, and a Council of Seventy, the church also has bishops, counselors, and teachers at all levels. Further, virtually all Mormon males serve as deacons and elders. Males over twelve years old are also members of the Mormon priesthood of Aaron or Melchizedek. Because they regard themselves as the true church, Mormons refer to all non-Mormons as "Gentiles."[8]

For the Mormons, their scriptures define their faith. They regard scripture as the Bible, *The Book of Mormon, Doctrines and Covenants,* and *The Pearl of Great Price.* Ken Boa summarizes the content of *The Book of Mormon,* the most important of the Mormon texts:

The *Book of Mormon*, which supposedly was written by several people from about 600 B.C. to A.D. 428, tells of the migration of an ancient people from the Tower of Babel to Central America. These people, known as the Jaredites, perished because of apostasy. A later migration occurred in 600 B.C. when a group of Jews were supposedly told by God to flee Jerusalem before the Babylonian captivity. These Jews, led by Lehi and his son Nephi, crossed the Pacific Ocean and landed in South America. There they divided into two opposing nations, the Nephites and the Lamanites. . . .

The Nephites recorded prophecies about the coming of Christ, and after His resurrection Christ visited them in South America. He instituted communion, baptism, and the priesthood for the Nephites. Later they were annihilated in a battle with the Lamanites in A.D. 428. Before they were killed in battle, Mormon, the compiler of the divinely revealed *Book of Mormon*, and his son Moroni took the golden plates on which "the revelation" was recorded and buried them. These plates were uncovered 1,400 years later by Joseph Smith.[9]

How reliable is this "history?" Several key points demonstrate that *The Book of Mormon* is unreliable as a historic text:

1. There are no reliable witnesses who saw the plates Smith supposedly translated.

2. As Boa remarks, "Though *The Book of Mormon* was buried in A.D. 428, it contains about 25,000 words verbatim from the A.D. 1611 King James version of the Bible!"[10]

3. I recently visited the new Mormon temple in Omaha, Nebraska, where I live. During the tour, one guest asked why there is no archeological evidence for the historical claims of *The Book of Mormon*. Our guide could offer no answer, but the extensive claims of the book would necessitate some kind of evidence for these peoples. There is none.

4. There is absolutely no evidence of anything called "reformed Egyptian hieroglyphics."

Mormonism is a worldview that has generated passion and incredible growth. It has been an aggressive religion, expecting all teens to commit two years to self-funded missionary service. Also, the LDS leaders expect every Mormon to tithe 10 percent of all income; the result is that the LDS church is extremely wealthy, with assets of over $30 billion.[11] Mormons are also visibly active in politics and social causes that promote conservative values and ethics. They remain a powerful force in American culture.

JEHOVAH'S WITNESSES, CHRISTIAN SCIENCE, AND MORMONISM: THEOLOGY AND ETHICS

God: Each of these cults views God differently; so here is a summary of each perspective.

1. *Jehovah's Witnesses* reject God as Trinitarian. God is one (called Jehovah), and the first being he created was Jesus Christ, who then created everything else. The Holy Spirit is an impersonal and active force of Jehovah.

2. *Christian Science* teaches that all matter is an illusion (as is sin, disease, and death) and that God is an impersonal principle of life, truth, intelligence, and spirit. God is "Divine Mind." The result is that God to the Christian Scientist is actually an impersonal, pantheistic force, thereby denying the Trinity and the deity of Christ.

3. *Mormonism* teaches that God the Father was once a man but became God. He has a physical body, as does his wife (the Heavenly Mother). Mormons deny the Trinity, arguing that the Father, Son, and Spirit are three separate gods. Mormons likewise teach that it is possible for all faithful Mormons to one day become gods too.

Jesus Christ: Each cult also has a different view of Jesus.

1. *Jehovah's Witnesses* teach that Jesus, while in heaven, was the archangel Michael, but that Jehovah, after creating him as Jesus Christ, made the physical universe through Him. He lived a perfect life on earth, and after dying on a stake (not a cross), He was resurrected as a spirit, and His body was destroyed. Jesus is "a god," not *the* God.

2. *Christian Science* teaches that Jesus was not God but lived the "Christ" (perfection) ideal. Because Christian Science teaches that all matter is an illusion, Jesus never became flesh and blood, never suffered for human sin on a cross, was not bodily resurrected, and is not coming again.

3. *Mormonism* teaches that Jesus is a separate god from the Father (Elohim) and is the spirit child of the Father and Mother in heaven. He is, therefore, the "elder brother" of all human spirit beings. His body was created through sexual union between Elohim and Mary. In fact, Mormonism teaches that Jesus was married, as a polygamist, to the two Marys and Martha. His death on Calvary's cross does not provide full atonement, but does guarantee resurrection for everyone.

Scripture: The Bible is important to each of these cults but is superseded or modified by other writings.

1. *Jehovah's Witnesses*—As mentioned in the historical review ear-

lier, the writings of the founder and early leaders (Russell and Rutherford) are important foundational teachings of this cult. However, today Witnesses also depend on the *New World Translation of the Holy Scriptures* and their magazines, *The Watchtower* and *Awake!*, to guide their thinking about doctrine and theology. The result is that they teach that the Bible cannot be understood without the guidance of the Zion Watchtower Society.

2. *Christian Science*—There is no question that Christian Science interprets the Bible through the works of Mary Baker Eddy, specifically *Science and Health, with Key to the Scriptures,* which is their real source of authority. Indeed, Eddy claimed that she was inspired by a direct revelation from God when she wrote *Science and Health,* considering it equal with the Bible. Boa reveals that she "believed she was the woman of Revelation 12 because she was being given the 'key to the Scriptures'."[12]

3. *Mormonism*—Without question, Mormons equate *The Book of Mormon: Another Testament of Jesus Christ* with the Bible; in fact, they regard it as more authoritative. The Book of Mormon is complemented by other texts, the *Pearl of Great Price* and *Doctrines and Covenants.*

Salvation: The similarity of these three cults is that each, in very different ways, promotes a works-righteousness view of salvation.

1. *Jehovah's Witnesses*—The first step is to be baptized as a Jehovah's Witness. But their core teaching is that followers merit everlasting life through door-to-door promotion of Witness beliefs. However, eternal life in heaven is limited to 144,000 "anointed ones" who have already been chosen by Jehovah. The remaining Witnesses who merit Jehovah's favor through their works will spend eternity on the rejuvenated earth, not in heaven.

2. *Christian Science*—Since humanity is not in a fallen state and because sin is an illusion, there is no real need for a savior. "Salvation" is thus mental deliverance from the error propagated by the illusions of the physical world—sickness, death, and evil. Christian Scientists seek that higher level of spiritual awareness that Mary Baker Eddy promised in her books. Victory over suffering and pain brings that spiritual awareness.

Mormonism—The LDS church actually defines "salvation" as an exaltation to godhood, which can only be earned through obedience to LDS leaders, Mormon baptism, tithing, marriage (which they believe is eternal), and secret temple rituals. Using 1 Corinthians 15:29, the LDS church also teaches that present-day Mormons can be vicariously baptized for their ancestors, who will then be "saved." For that reason,

Mormons spend a great deal of time studying their family's genealogy so that they can be baptized in their place.[13]

BUILDING BRIDGES TO THE CULTS

Because there is so much complexity in dealing with these three different cults, here are three basic bridges that we can build to reach their followers with the gospel of Jesus Christ.

Bridge #1

Each one of these cults has a strong commitment to the spiritual realm beyond the physical. Each believes it is possible to connect with this spiritual world through the specific activities of the believer. As Bible-centered Christians, we believe that as well, but we must explain clearly that a relationship with God is possible only through Jesus Christ (John 14:6). In effect, as we build a relationship with cult members, we must keep coming back to Jesus—He is the only Way! Through our lifestyle and our words, we can demonstrate that truth. Jehovah's Witnesses, Christian Scientists, and Mormons all believe in a spiritual world, but they simply do not have certainty on how to get there.

Bridge #2

Each one of these cults also believes in the Bible. Each cult reads the Bible but through the lens of cult beliefs. Each has other books to explain what the Bible teaches. The Bible is not enough for them. We must be ready to demonstrate an apologetic for the Bible as the unique Word of God. We must also be prepared to use God's Word to demonstrate the deity of Jesus, the unique saving work of Jesus, and the clear understanding that salvation is through faith in Jesus, not through works. It is important to keep the focus on God's Word, not on their books. If they do not want to discuss the Bible, then do not get engaged in a conversation about their written works unless you have adequately studied them. Remember, it is not your job to change a cult member; that is God's business. Your job is to be a faithful witness of the truth revealed in the Bible.

Bridge #3

As with Christianity, each one of these cults calls for an intense commitment. Few Mormons joined the LDS church because they were drawn initially to *The Book of Mormon.* Few Christian Scientists joined

Christian Science because they were drawn to Eddy's *Science and Health*. Jehovah's Witnesses initially drawn to the Zion Watchtower Society didn't join because they read the *New World Translation*. The appeal of the cults is quite simple. Each cult meets basic human needs: the need to belong, to have fellowship, to have a sense of identity and purpose, to be affirmed as a person, to have answers for life's enduring problems. Also many join one of the cults because of the need for authority and certainty in their lives. In most cults, there is little ambiguity.

Therefore, we must not only be willing to demonstrate the trustworthiness of the Bible and the uniqueness of Jesus Christ, but also the authenticity and genuineness of biblical Christianity. The fruit of the Spirit (Gal. 5:22-23) are powerful manifestations of that authenticity. Christians must also show the same intense commitment to Jesus and to truth that cultists show to their ideology. We have the answers, and we have the truth. The supernatural nature of our "walk" must match the power of our words.

In Acts 17:16-34, the apostle Paul met the Athenian philosophers on their own turf. He recognized their spiritual need, recognized their religiosity, and recognized their quest for truth; but he demonstrated the inadequacy of all of these by pointing them correctly to Jesus. That must be our methodology as we seek to build bridges to the cults.[14]

FOR FURTHER DISCUSSION

1. Identify common themes in the characteristics and history of the three cults of this chapter.
2. What has been your experience or what observations can you make related to members of these three cults?
3. Name reasons why the Bible is more reliable than the supplemental holy books of each cult.
4. How does each cult studied in this chapter view the following:
   • God
   • Jesus
   • salvation
5. What are some key points from the chapter that you will keep in mind the next time you talk to a member of one of these cults?
6. Why is it important to stay focused on Jesus and the Bible when witnessing to cult members?

11

Roman Catholicism, Protestantism, and Eastern Orthodoxy: What's the Difference?

TODAY WHEN SOMEONE uses the term "Christian" to describe their religious convictions or worship preferences, it is no longer clear what that means. There is Roman Catholic Christianity, Eastern Orthodox Christianity with its multifaceted liturgy and divisions (Greek, Russian, Serbian, etc.), and Protestant Christianity with its many denominational structures and worship styles. How do we evaluate and understand these various expressions of Christianity? What aspects do they have in common? Where do the doctrinal differences lie?

The way to answer these questions is to understand the historical background and development of each one. This chapter will trace this development, stressing the historical and doctrinal differences of each and concluding with bridges to Eastern Orthodoxy and Roman Catholicism. Since both traditions are expressions of Christianity, the bridges will not necessarily be for evangelistic purposes, as in previous chapters. Rather, they will give some points of connection, or commonalities, between Protestants, Roman Catholics, and Eastern Orthodox Christians and some points for dialogue about the differences, including places for mutual learning. The goal is to build relationships centered on biblical truth with Christian individuals from different traditions. Because I am an evangelical Protestant, I am evaluating Orthodoxy and Catholicism from that perspective.

By way of introduction, it is imperative to remember how much

Vatican II changed the Roman Catholic church. Called initially by Pope John XXIII, Vatican II was a Council of 2,500 bishops who met in four sessions from 1962 through 1965. In effect, this Council reconciled Catholicism with the modern world. It permitted the Mass to be said in the language of the people instead of only in Latin. It endorsed a more positive attitude toward Protestants and Jews. Perhaps most important, it encouraged the laity to study Scripture for themselves under a priest's guidance and to play a greater role in the church. Finally, it insisted on the necessity of religious liberty, especially on issues of conscience. The result nearly forty years later is that Catholicism is actually a spectrum, with those who affirm the traditional Latin-oriented Mass and historic Catholicism on the one end and evangelical/charismatic/Pentecostal Catholics on the other. This chapter recognizes this diversity within the church but focuses its theological analysis on the official statements of theology within that church.

THE HISTORY OF CHRISTIANITY: CATHOLICISM, ORTHODOXY, AND THE ORIGIN OF PROTESTANTISM

The Origins of Roman Catholicism

The Christian church began on Pentecost when the Holy Spirit filled the nearly 120 believers gathered in Jerusalem. From there it spread to Judea, Samaria, and then to the uttermost parts of the earth (Acts 1:8). Organizationally, the church developed from a plurality of church leadership in the first century (e.g., Phil. 1:1), to a bishop having authority over several churches in the second century, to a hierarchical structure in the third and fourth centuries. By the fifth century, the church regarded the Bishop of Rome as the first among equals and the city of Rome as its geographical center. Through church councils (c.f., Nicea in 325, Chalcedon in 451, and others), the church agreed that the Bible taught that God is Trinitarian, Jesus is God, His death is a substitutionary one, and He is coming again.

Protestant church historians generally maintain that institutionalized Roman Catholicism began with Gregory's appointment as bishop of Rome in A.D. 590. Though he refused the title of pope, administratively, he organized the papal system of government that characterized the entire medieval period. Thus, all the major bishoprics of the West looked to him for guidance and leadership. He likewise standardized the liturgy and theology of the burgeoning Roman church. Doctrines such as the veneration of Mary, purgatory, an early form of transubstantiation, and praying to departed saints found their initial pronouncements in his writings.

Gregory also promoted missionary activity among the Germanic tribes who had conquered the western Roman Empire and now needed to hear the gospel. Gregory's zeal for missions led him to send dozens of monks to northern Europe, especially to England. Many in England came to Christ, and Canterbury became the English center of Catholicism. Bishop Gregory laid the foundation for the great edifice known as Roman Catholicism.

Two other factors contributed to the growing power and prestige of the Roman bishop. First, an early king of the Franks, Pepin the Short (741-768), granted the pope extensive land in central Italy—the Donation of Pepin—making the Catholic church a temporal and political power in Europe. Second, the Donation of Constantine allegedly gave power and authority to the Roman bishop when Constantine relocated his capital to the East. That document was later discovered to be a forgery. Both, however, solidified the power of the pope.

Missionary activity throughout Europe by Boniface (672-754), Columba (521-597), Patrick (ca. 389-461), and many others brought the areas under Germanic tribal domination into the Roman Catholic fold. The church became a civilizing force as these tribes converted to faith.

During the medieval period of church history (600-1500), a group of theologians called the scholastics systematized the body of critical Roman Catholic doctrine. Anselm (1033-1109) gave reasonable proofs for God's existence and compelling reasons for God as the self-existent, incorporeal, almighty, compassionate, just, and merciful one. In his book *Why the Godman?* Anselm also demonstrated the crucial interrelationship between the incarnation of God's Son and His atonement for sin.

The apex of scholastic theology, however, was reached with Thomas Aquinas. His life of scholarship forever shaped the direction of institutionalized Catholicism. In his *Summa Theologica*, he gave critical support to the distinctive doctrines of the Christian faith, including the attributes of God, the Resurrection, and *ex nihilo* creation. He also defended the veneration of Mary, purgatory, the seven holy sacraments through which God conveys grace, and the role of human merit in salvation—all distinctive Roman Catholic doctrines. Aquinas likewise gave a philosophical defense that the Communion elements at the prayer of consecration become, sacrificially, the actual body and blood of Christ (transubstantiation). Roman Catholicism not only had a distinct hierarchical structure with clear geographical support, but it now had a defining theology that was being defended.[1]

The Split between Western Catholicism and Eastern Orthodoxy

The division of the church between East and West is rooted deeply in church history. Early on, the church leaders noticed the difference and discrepancies that language presented. The Eastern church spoke and wrote Greek, while the West began to speak and write in Latin. This was perhaps the first sign of division within the church.

Several additional developments enhanced the separation that was clearly geographical and lingual. First, when Pepin made his donation of land in central Italy to the papacy in 756, the pope naturally fixed his attention more on the West, essentially ignoring the East. Second, Pepin's son Charlemagne came to Rome and on Christmas Day, 800, was formally crowned Holy Roman Emperor by Pope Leo III. This act symbolized the division of East and West.

A doctrinal development further intensified the East-West division. The issue centered on the question: Who sent the Holy Spirit—the Father or the Father and the Son? The great fifth-century theologian Augustine (354-430) argued strongly that the Spirit was sent ("proceeded from") both the Father and the Son. In 589, at a Western council that met in Toledo, Spain, Western theologians added to the Nicene Creed of 381 the language that the Spirit proceeded from the Father and the Son (in Latin *filioque,* which means "and from the Son"). This controversy is hence called the *filioque* controversy. The Eastern theologians strongly protested this addition.

Another theological controversy separating East and West was the dating of Easter. During the first several centuries of the church, Eastern Christians celebrated Easter on Passover. The West always celebrated Easter on a Sunday. At the 325 Council of Nicea, the Eastern practice was condemned, thereby marking another divergence.

Other historical developments magnified the East-West split. First, in 858 Pope Nicholas reversed the appointment of Photius as the Eastern patriarch of Constantinople. Eastern Christians regarded this as yet another encroachment upon their autonomy. Second, in 876 an Eastern church synod in Constantinople (modern-day Istanbul) condemned the Western pope for his increasing political activities as a secular ruler of Italian land and for his failure to correct what they called the heresy of the *filioque* clause. This synod symbolized the entire East's rejection of the pope's claim of universal jurisdiction over the church.

The most noticeable break, or what came to be known as the Great Schism, happened in 1054. On June 16th of that year, Pope Leo IX excommunicated Orthodox Patriarch Michael Cerularius for "trying to humiliate and crush the holy catholic and apostolic church." The patriarch then excommunicated Pope Leo. This mutual excommunication marks the formal break between Eastern and Western Christianity that has lasted to this day.[2]

The hostility and split were further intensified when, during the 1204 crusade, the crusaders sacked and pillaged Constantinople on Good Friday. So horrific and inexcusable was this event that the break between Eastern and Western Christianity was final and complete.

Islam also had a devastating effect on the Eastern church. Major centers of the Eastern church—Jerusalem, Antioch, and Alexandria— fell into Muslim hands, and after the eighth century theological development in these areas ceased. Therefore, leadership of the Eastern church gravitated to Constantinople's patriarch. When that city fell to the Muslim Ottoman Turks in 1453, leadership passed to the Russian Orthodox patriarch, who declared that Moscow would be the "Third Rome," after historic Rome and Constantinople. Today, in effect, there are thirteen self-governing and independent churches in Eastern Orthodoxy, each with its own leader—either a patriarch, archbishop, or metropolitan.

The Split Between Western Catholicism and Protestant Christianity

The Roman Catholic church experienced a crisis of authority during the fourteenth and fifteenth centuries. Upheaval within and remarkable pressures from without undermined its credibility and legitimacy. Several developments heightened this crisis:

• From 1309-1378, due to political and religious controversies, there were in effect two popes, one in Rome and one in Avignon, France. Attempts to settle this unacceptable situation further divided church leaders and harmed the church's leadership.

• In addition, the church was racked by corruption and fraud. Clergy bought and sold offices (simony). Immorality among church leaders who professed celibacy elevated the crisis of confidence. The church likewise spent a fortune acquiring thousands of relics for its cathedrals and paying for them with the sale of forgiveness (indulgences). The church thus became an object of ridicule and satire in pamphlets and books readily available due to the invention of the printing press.

• In the fourteenth and fifteenth centuries, mystics such as the Brethren of Common Life, rejecting the scholastic coldness and legalism of the church, emphasized obedience, holiness, and simplicity through meditation, confession of sin, and the imitation of Christ.

• Availability of the Word of God further undermined the church. John Wycliffe (ca. 1329-1384) believed that the Bible was the final authority for the believer and that each believer should have an opportunity to read it. He and his followers translated the Latin Vulgate into English.

• Finally, modern nation-states challenged the church for supremacy, and the voyages of discovery made the earth appear smaller. Further, the Renaissance of northern Italy caused many to abandon Catholicism in favor of the glories of ancient Greece and Rome.

Into the volatile sixteenth century stepped Martin Luther (1483-1546). After his education in law and theology, he accepted a teaching position at a small university at Wittenberg, Germany. There he challenged the church on its sale of indulgences. On October 31, 1517, he nailed his Ninety-five Theses for debate to the Castle Church door at Wittenberg. Those theses and subsequent events set off a firestorm within the church that led to his excommunication and the formation of the Lutheran church. Among many other things, Luther and his followers rejected the dogma of transubstantiation, argued for the sole authority of Scripture, and advocated justification by faith alone.

Luther's followers increased, and at the German Imperial Diet at Speyer in 1529, those who dissented due to the church's clampdown on religious renewal were called "Protestants." That name has since characterized all religious groups during the Reformation that left the Catholic church. Throughout the Holy Roman Empire, towns removed religious statues, abolished the Mass, and forced priests from churches. The Reformation had become political as well as religious.

In Switzerland two major leaders emerged to lay the foundation for the Reformed tradition—Ulrich Zwingli (1484-1531) and John Calvin (1509-1564). Each married, demonstrating like Luther that spiritual leadership did not demand celibacy. Zwingli died young, but

Calvin's influence extended to the Presbyterian John Knox (1514-1572), the Dutch Reformation, the English Reformation, and the Pilgrims and Puritans who would take Protestantism to North America. Because Calvin believed so strongly in the sovereignty of God, he held that God was directly involved in all aspects of the drama of salvation, including predestination and election. Today Calvinism is found in historic Presbyterianism, Reformed faiths, and some Baptist groups.

Anabaptism was another influential aspect of the Protestant Reformation. As a term, *anabaptist* means "to again baptize." As a movement, Anabaptism stressed believer's baptism, as opposed to infant baptism. But the term also refers to widely diverse groups of Reformers, many of whom embraced quite radical social, political, economic, and religious views. The most respectable Anabaptist groups included the Swiss Brethren, the Mennonites, and the Amish. Other distinctives of Anabaptism include a commitment to the gathered church concept as opposed to the state church. Therefore, many called for the separation of church and state. Many also advocated the position of nonresistance and even pacifism.

In Britain and America other Protestant denominational groups developed. In the mid-to-late 1700s the Methodists, under John Wesley, broke from the state-supported Anglican church and preached revival throughout England and America. The Baptists, who stressed believer's baptism, spread across America. They followed the teachings of John Arminius, which stressed human free will and the importance of trusting Christ for salvation. In America the Black church, originating out of the slave religion of the South, grew and began to organize into denominations as early as 1816.

In early twentieth-century America, the Pentecostal movement was born. This movement, first institutionalized in the Assembly of God churches in 1916, emphasized the spiritual gifts of healing and speaking in tongues. It evolved through the century in many ways, each facet stressing one or more of the sign gifts. In Asia, Latin America, Africa, and the United States it remains a formidable Protestant and Catholic force in the church today.

Since Protestantism broke from the Catholic church through the sixteenth century Reformation, it has continued to fragment and divide. Today denominationalism is the chief characteristic of the multiple expressions of Protestant Christianity.[3]

ROMAN CATHOLICISM AND EASTERN ORTHODOXY: THEOLOGY AND ETHICS

Roman Catholicism

Theologically, the Roman Catholic church has consistently held to the historical and biblical view of the Trinity—God as Father, Son, and Holy Spirit. Equally, the church has defended the deity of Jesus Christ and His virgin birth. However, Catholics and Protestants have differed in several areas.

Scripture: The official position of the Roman Catholic church is that "Sacred Tradition and Sacred Scripture" are equal sources of authority for the Christian. The church is entrusted with the transmission and interpretation of these two authorities, and it declares what that revelation from God says and means. Tradition for the Roman Catholic refers to the external dogmatic authority that resides in the teaching "magisterium of the church" as expressed in the primacy and infallibility of the papacy. "Both Scripture and Tradition must be accepted and honored with equal sentiments of devotion and reverence."[4]

Mary: The Catholic church teaches that Mary is the "mother of God," who was immaculately conceived (that is born without original sin) and instead of dying, was bodily taken to heaven (the Assumption of Mary). Therefore, the church teaches that "the Holy Mother of God, the new Eve, Mother of the Church, continues in heaven to exercise her maternal role on behalf of the members of Christ."[5]

Sacraments: The Catholic church teaches that there are seven grace-conveying sacraments—baptism, confirmation, the Eucharist (or Communion), penance, Extreme Unction (last rites), holy orders, and marriage. Although the church baptizes adults when they convert to Catholicism, it practices infant baptism to cleanse the child of original sin. The church also teaches baptismal regeneration (i.e., that baptism is necessary for salvation). For the church, the Eucharist centers on transubstantiation. Catholics believe that during the prayer of consecration made by the priest, the bread and the wine literally become the body and blood of Jesus. Each time the Mass is said, Jesus is sacrificially present in the elements.[6]

Salvation: For the Roman Catholic church, salvation is more of a process than an event—a line not a point. That process begins with infant baptism and is nourished throughout life by the sacraments. The church teaches that after baptism the believer will continue to sin.

However, there are two categories of sin: (1) *Mortal sin,* which can cause a person to lose sanctifying grace and thereby separates the person from God. Forgiveness for mortal sin can come only through confession to a priest or an act of repentance. (2) *Venial sins* are less serious and do not take away grace. They are removed by simple acts of repentance.

The church teaches that faith is merely the beginning of salvation, for the believer must work throughout life to complete the process begun by faith. The faithful Catholic must follow the sacraments regularly. If he or she neglects the sacraments, or if mortal or venial sins are committed, and there is no confession, then the believer who dies in this condition will spend time in purgatory. In purgatory, believers can receive temporal punishment for sin that then purifies them for heaven.[7]

Eastern Orthodoxy

Daniel Clendenin describes a typical Orthodox worship service: "The near absence of chairs or pews, dim lighting, head coverings for most women, icons and frescoes covering almost every inch of space on the walls and ceiling, a massive and ornate iconostasis separating the priest and the worshipers, the smoky smell of incense and hundreds of candles burning in memory of the dead, the priest resplendent in his ornate vestments and enormous beard, and worshipers repeatedly prostrating themselves, kissing the icons, and making the sign of the cross."[8] What are the beliefs of Orthodoxy that produce a worship service often so foreign to Western Protestants?

The Church: Eastern Orthodoxy teaches that it is the one true church on earth, tracing its origins back to the apostolic church in unbroken succession. The implication of this position is that both Catholics and Protestants have departed from the true church and the true faith.

The Sacraments: As with the Roman Catholic church, Eastern Orthodoxy affirms the seven sacraments through which God transmits both saving and sanctifying grace. Baptism, however, is the primary sacrament, for "everything in the church flows out of the waters of baptism: the remission of sin and life eternal."[9] Orthodoxy practices infant baptism, immersing the child three times, by which the infant is "born again" and wholly cleansed from all sin. Immediately following baptism is the rite of "chrismation." The priest anoints the child with a special ointment, making the sign of the cross on various parts of the body, symbolizing the gift and seal of the Holy Spirit.

Like Catholicism, Orthodoxy teaches the sacrificial presence of Jesus in the Communion elements, but Orthodoxy rejects transubstantiation, simply affirming the mystery of the sacrament. Orthodoxy also administers Communion to infants.

Icons: Probably the most unusual aspect of Orthodoxy for the Protestant is the centrality of icons during worship. At baptism the believer often receives an icon of the saint whose name he or she takes; at marriage the fathers of the couple bless them with icons; and at death the icon precedes the burial procession. Icons are flat images of Christ, Mary, or a saint. These usually take the form of wooden pictures painted in oils and are often ornately decorated with brilliant colors.

The icons are central to Orthodoxy because they are of equal benefit and mutually revelatory with the written Word. Icons are not idols or vile images. They are types, figures, and shadows of the truths of Christianity. What the Bible proclaims in words, the icon proclaims in color. For the Eastern Orthodox Christian, icons demonstrate the humanity of Jesus, which is the key to His incarnation. The icons of Jesus demonstrate that He is God and man together in one person localized in space-time history. Icons thus teach a profound truth of Christianity.

Theosis: One of the most difficult Orthodox doctrines to understand is that of "theosis" (deification). Orthodoxy teaches that "As human beings we each have this one unique calling, to achieve Theosis. In other words, we each are destined to become a god; to be like God Himself, to be united with Him. . . . (2 Pet. 1:4). This is the purpose of your life . . . to become just like God, a true God."[10] For Orthodoxy, this astonishing doctrine does not mean that humans become or join the essence of God (as in pantheism); rather humans remain distinctly human by nature "but participate in God by divine energies or grace. At no point, even when deified, is our humanity diminished or destroyed."[11] Synonyms for this Orthodox teaching might be transformation, co-mingling, assimilation, or an "influx of the divine."[12]

Scripture: For the Protestant, Scripture is the final authority. For the Roman Catholic, both Scripture and tradition have authority. However, for the Eastern Orthodox, theological authority is internal, coming from the Spirit Who speaks to believers through tradition. For Orthodoxy, the papacy is not the guardian of truth, the "whole people of God is the protector of apostolic tradition."[13] As Clendenin argues, "tradition is the life of the Spirit in the church, who alone is the ultimate criterion of truth."[14] For that reason, since the Bible is the unique expression of that tradition, it is elevated, incensed, kissed, and given a place of honor in various processions. However, tradition also includes the historic church councils and the early church fathers and their writings. Orthodox believers never approach Scripture without filtering it through the grid provided by the councils and the fathers. They are all complementary in the Spirit's witness to truth.

Other Differences with Roman Catholicism

Where the Catholic church affirms purgatory, Orthodoxy repudiates this belief. Where the Catholic church demands celibacy of all its clergy, Orthodoxy permits clergy below the office of bishop to marry. Where the Catholic church affirms the Bishop of Rome (the pope) as head of the church, Orthodoxy repudiates that teaching. Orthodoxy mandates its clergy wear beards, while that is not an issue in Catholicism.

Roman Catholicism and Eastern Orthodoxy strongly agree on the foundational doctrine of the Trinitarian godhead. But when it comes to almost all other manifestations of faith and practice, they differ, often considerably. Both of these Christian traditions also differ rather radically from historic Protestantism. Building any bridges between the three expressions is challenging. However, a focus on the commonalities between all three expressions, a respectful yet firm dialogue about the differences, and a humility and openness to learn from each other are essential for building mutually beneficial, cooperative, and respectful relationships with individuals from all three traditions.

BUILDING BRIDGES TO ROMAN CATHOLICS AND EASTERN ORTHODOXY

Bridge #1

Both Roman Catholicism and Eastern Orthodoxy affirm a belief in the Trinitarian God. Each believe that God is one essence of three persons— Father, Son, and Holy Spirit. Agreement on this truth becomes a central starting point for both appreciating and understanding each Christian tradition. This agreement is also the starting point in building relationships with Christians from different traditions.

Bridge #2

Both Catholicism and Orthodoxy affirm the deity and redemptive work of Jesus Christ to save humankind from sin. They agree with Protestantism's emphasis on the centrality of the cross for Christianity. There can be no stronger connection than this! The incarnation, crucifixion, resurrection, and glorification of our King of Kings and Lord of Lords is the common heartbeat of every Christian church. This connection should never be minimized.

Bridge #3

All three expressions of Christianity share a common historic tradition. In fact, both Catholicism and Orthodoxy often have a greater respect for church history and the Christian tradition that has developed through history than evangelical Protestants. Evangelical Protestants often have the conviction that they are the first ones to discover truths from Scripture, when in reality most truths have been discovered before, probably during the first few hundred years of church history. This respect for and acknowledgment of the Christian historic tradition is an important link between all expressions of Christianity. We are all on common ground here, a fact that evangelical Protestants especially need to recognize.

Bridge #4

Fourth, Scripture is held in high regard in both Catholicism and Orthodoxy. Although there is disagreement as to the level of authority placed on Scripture, each tradition honors Scripture and accepts it as a reliable source of Christian doctrine and practice. This is an important starting place in framing discussions centered on biblical truth.

POINTS FOR DIALOGUE AND MUTUAL LEARNING

Although there are several commonalities between the three expressions of Christianity, there are also many differences that cannot be minimized. First, one of the major doctrinal differences is the understanding of exactly how salvation occurs. Protestant teaching is that justification (i.e., salvation) is solely by faith. Both Catholicism and Orthodoxy teach that human works, usually through the sacraments, are needed to, in the end, merit God's favor. It is therefore justification by faith plus human works. This belief contradicts the entire book of

Galatians and the simplicity of teaching in Ephesians 2:8-9. Justification by faith alone was the central message of the Reformation and remains the major difference between biblical Protestant Christianity and Catholicism and Orthodoxy.

However, on the other hand, Protestants would benefit from placing more value on good works. Justification is immediate, but sanctification is a lifelong process. Although works do not merit God's favor, sometimes Protestants minimize works so much that their spirituality becomes lazy and is only "fire insurance" for staying out of hell. Good works should be held in high regard as the fruits and proof of salvation.

A second area of dialogue is church tradition. Catholics and Orthodox Christians emphasize tradition while Protestants often minimize it. For Protestants, an increased appreciation of the Christian historic tradition would provide an accurate understanding of the complexities and richness of historic Christianity. As we understand the diversity and the contributions many individuals and groups have made to the church, we become more tolerant and appreciative of groups with which we may personally disagree. Such humility can be a real growth point for us as evangelical Protestants. It likewise provides a basis for very meaningful dialogue between evangelical Protestants, Catholics, and Orthodoxy. Hopefully that dialogue will also help the Catholic and Orthodox Christian see that historical tradition is not to be idolized, but is a source of help in solving the difficulties of the present. We can learn from the past, but we are not frozen in the past. Catholicism and Orthodoxy need to learn that truth.

The Catholic and Orthodox expressions of Christianity are difficult for the Protestant evangelical to understand and identify with. We certainly can learn from them, but God can use us to emphasize the truth to them that their faith is centered in the person of Jesus and His finished work on Calvary's cross. Appropriating that finished work by faith is how justification occurs. For many Catholic and Orthodox Christians, their allegiance to tradition has kept them from seeing that central truth.

FOR FURTHER DISCUSSION

1. What new perspectives have you gained about each of the Christian traditions from a review of its history? What do you see as low points and high points in these histories?
2. What historical events and figures do you see as most important in shaping current church traditions and practices today?

3. Summarize the theological differences between Catholicism and Protestantism about the following:
   - Scripture
   - Mary
   - salvation
   - sacraments
4. What was most interesting or surprising to you about Eastern Orthodoxy? Explain the meaning behind icons and the doctrine of Theosis.
5. Summarize the different views of each of the three groups on Scripture and tradition. How might Scripture be used as a bridge?
6. Where do you see your need to learn from other Christian traditions? What bridge or bridges will you use as you seek to form Bible-based relationships with your Catholic and Orthodox friends?

12

Christianity as a Worldview

CHRISTIANITY IS NOT ONLY a personal relationship with the living God through faith in Jesus Christ; it is a worldview. It is an entire way of thinking, covering not only theology, but how to think about ethics, history, science, literature—about everything. Because God has revealed Himself verbally in the Bible, Christians have the answers to the most penetrating questions of life. James W. Sire suggests that there are seven such basic questions, similar to the worldview questions we have been seeking to answer throughout this book:

1. What is prime reality—the really real?
2. What is the nature of external reality, i.e., outside of ourselves?
3. What is a human being?
4. What happens to a person at death?
5. Why is it possible to know anything at all?
6. How do we know what is right and wrong?
7. What is the meaning of history?

Human beings must come to terms with these questions at some time during their life. Sire argues that to discover one's worldview is a "significant step toward self-awareness, self-knowledge, and self-understanding."[1]

This book has been a brief survey of the major worldviews currently dominant in our world today. Each worldview has a significant portion of humanity convinced that it is the legitimate worldview. After reviewing briefly the history and theology of each and how to build bridges to each, I am concluding the book with a rigorous presentation of genuine biblical Christianity as a worldview. By the phrase "genuine biblical Christianity," I mean the faith clearly revealed in God's Word, the Bible, and which has been validated through human history.

God: Biblical Christianity views God as He is revealed in the Bible; one of those central truths is the doctrine of the Trinity. It separates biblical Christianity from all other worldviews.

The Bible teaches in Deuteronomy 6:4 that God is one; yet from the New Testament it is clear that this one God consists of three persons—Father, Son, and Holy Spirit. The church has always affirmed this doctrine as orthodox, but wrestling with its theological and philosophical implications has always been a challenge. Especially in the early church, this struggle often produced heresy, and it continues to do so today (e.g., the Jehovah's Witnesses and Mormonism).

The ancient church of the third and fourth centuries was plagued with false teaching that challenged the deity of Jesus and the Holy Spirit, whether it was the teachings of Arius (who denied Jesus' deity) or the Pneumatomachians, who believed that the Son and the Spirit were subordinate to the Father. In order to preserve the oneness of God, others argued that Jesus was a man who was *adopted* as the Son of God; thus He was not eternally the Son. Others contended there was one God who revealed Himself in one of three modes—Father, Son, and Spirit.

The critical question has always been, "What does Scripture teach?" More specifically, what precise, descriptive words will guard against heresy when it comes to the relationship between the Father, Son, and Spirit? The biblical teaching on God as Trinity argues that we must always separate the terms *essence* and *person;* they are not synonyms. *Essence* is what makes God, God. Attributes such as omnipotence, omnipresence, and omniscience are encompassed here. *Person* is a term that defines the distinctions within that one essence. Thus we can correctly say "God the Father," "God the Son," and "God the Holy Spirit," while maintaining that they are one and inseparable in being. Yet the difference between each can be grounded only in relational and functional differences. Any language that results in the Son's or Spirit's subordination to the Father is simply unacceptable.

Thus, by definition, the Trinity is one God of three persons whose difference is relational and functional, not essential. We do not have three gods or three modes of God; we have one God. Ephesians 1:1-14 illustrates this truth quite well—the Father chooses, the Son redeems, the Spirit seals (see also 2 Cor. 13:14; 1 Pet. 1:2). Each member of the Godhead is intimately involved in the drama of salvation. We thus can join Paul and praise the Trinitarian God of grace.[2]

God is also revealed in Scripture as the creator and sustainer of all life. As prime reality, God creates *ex nihilo* and then sustains all that He creates (see Gen. 1—2; Col. 1:15-20). He is a God of truth (John 14:6), and His revelation (i.e., the written Word) is truth (John 17:17). He is a personal God who seeks intimacy and fellowship with His creatures (see the Psalms, 1 John and John 4). Atheism, pantheism, or polytheism are not viable options for understanding God as the prime reality.

Jesus: Without question, the defining issue of biblical Christianity is Jesus Christ. Only a Jesus who is truly God and truly man can provide complete salvation for humanity. He must be fully human to be our substitute, and He must be fully God to be our perfect substitute. For that reason biblical Christianity has always taught that Jesus is both God and man—the Godman.

Since He is both God and man in one person, how does His deity and His humanity relate to each other? Both natures are joined in a miraculous way so that neither is damaged, diminished, or impaired. He is, then, an undiminished deity plus perfect humanity united in one person, without any confusion of the two natures. In that absolute sense, He is the Godman! Therefore, when describing Jesus, any choice of words that diminishes His deity or His humanity (e.g., Mormonism and Jehovah's Witnesses) is incorrect and heretical. A complete salvation demands it; faith in the Godman, Jesus Christ, procures it.[3]

Salvation: Biblical Christianity declares that humans are born sinners and inherit the guilt and corruption of Adam, for when Adam sinned, all sinned (Rom. 5:12). Therefore, the fundamental problem of the human race is not political, social, economic, or psychological; it is spiritual. Following the apostle Paul's articulation in Romans and Galatians of the human problem of sin, the Bible gives the solution as the free-grace gospel of Jesus Christ. God's grace is thus absolutely essential for human salvation, and that grace is magnified in Jesus.

How does one appropriate God's grace in Jesus? Only by faith in His finished work on Calvary's cross. Because God is just and holy, He demands payment for sin. Further, any human action or work to merit God's favor in salvation is inadequate—all human righteousness is as "filthy rags" (Isa. 64:6). The situation, therefore, appears hopeless. Because of this hopeless human condition and because of His love, God sent the second Person of the Trinity to add a human nature to His divine nature and die on the cross as our substitute (Isa. 52:13—53:12; John 3:16). God's just demands are thus met and we appropriate that finished work through faith (Eph. 2:8-9). We then become His children by adoption into His family with all the rights, benefits, and privileges intact (Gal. 4:1-7).

For that reason, any worldview that adds something to faith contradicts biblical teaching. Every worldview covered in this book, whether the major world religions or the cults, declares that human works in some form are necessary to merit the favor of deity. God's Word is very clear that no human work can merit salvation. In terms of salvation, any teaching that adds to or substitutes for the finished work of Jesus Christ, the apostle Paul calls "another gospel" (Gal. 1:6-7) and is regarded as heretical.

Ethics: This book has demonstrated that ethical human behavior is tied to worldview. Whether one worships the gods of the world religions or the heretical gods of the cults, worldview determines ethical behavior. The thesis of this section is that biblical Christianity roots ethics in God's moral law as revealed in His Word.

Erwin Lutzer makes this compelling argument: "If naturalism is false and if theism is true, and therefore God is responsible for all that is, then revelation is possible. And if revelation is possible, then absolute standards are possible, should the Deity choose to make them known."[4]

Has God chosen to make such standards known? The resounding answer of biblical Christianity is yes. He has chosen to reveal Himself in His Son (Heb. 1:1-4), through His creation (Ps. 19; Rom. 1:18ff.), and through His Word (Ps. 119; 2 Tim. 3:16; 2 Pet. 1:21), and we know about the Son through the Word. These propositional truths form the basis for ethical absolutes.

What are these propositional truths that constitute the Christian ethical framework?

1. *God's moral revelation in His Word is an expression of His own nature.* He is holy, and therefore He insists that His human creatures also meet that standard. If they do not, judgment results. Hence, the vital nature of Jesus' substitutionary atonement. Appropriating that atoning work by faith makes the human holy in God's eyes, and thus acceptable to God. The same argument can be made about God's ethical standards of truth, beauty, love, life, and sexuality.

2. *God's moral and ethical system consists of more than external conformity to His moral code; it centers on conformity with internal issues of motivation and personal attitudes.* Jesus' teaching in the Sermon on the Mount presses this point. The ethical standard prohibiting adultery involves more than simply the external act; it also involves lusting with the heart after someone (Matt. 5:27-28). The prohibition of murder

involves more than the external act; it includes bitterness, hatred, and anger in the heart (Matt. 5:21-22).

3. *God provides the absolute criteria for determining the value of human beings.* Because physical, economic, mental, and social/cultural criteria are all arbitrary and relative, they are inadequate for assigning value to humans. God created humans in His image (Gen. 1:26ff.) and established His absolute criteria for their value. Being made in the image of God means that humans *resemble* God. Like God, humans possess self-consciousness, self-will, and moral responsibility. What humans lost in the Fall (Gen. 3) was righteousness, holiness, and knowledge; these are renewed in Christians as they are being conformed to the image of Christ. Being in God's image also means that humans *represent* God. God's purpose in creating human beings is functional (Gen. 1:26-27). Humans have the responsibility of dominion over creation and of being fruitful and multiplying. Humans represent God as His stewards over His world. This concept is emphasized in Genesis 2 and reiterated in Psalms 8 and 110. Humans are God's vice-regents over all creation with power to control, regulate, and harness its potential. The Fall did not abolish this stewardship. Instead, Satan is the usurper and enemy of humans in their dominion status. Man lives out of harmony with himself and with nature. Created to rule, humans find that the crown has fallen from their brows.[5]

History: Biblical Christianity offers an approach to history rooted in God's revelation. Past historical perspectives offer little help today. The ancient Greeks adhered to a cyclical philosophy of history that saw past events as a series of repetitive cycles—the old adage that history repeats itself. The religions of Hinduism, Buddhism, and the amorphous New Age Movement, with their common emphasis on reincarnation, all view history similarly. The common element among them all is an absence of hope, meaning, and purpose.

Other approaches to history are inadequate as well. The eighteenth-century Enlightenment saw history through the grid of progress. The Scientific Revolution of the preceding century and the certainty of constructing a science of man created an optimism about humanity that viewed human perfectibility as imminent. Destroyed by the carnage of the twentieth century (two World Wars and the Holocaust), the view of progress is no longer viable. Modern existentialism or postmodernism offer no meaning to history except individual autonomy and choice.

Biblical Christianity's approach, rooted in God's revelation, gives hope and solid confidence for the future. This approach has four essential aspects:

First, the Bible calls for a worldview that rejects the cyclical model of history. The ancient Hebrews saw history as a line with a beginning, a middle, and an end. Creation marked the initiation of history with God creating the universe *ex nihilo*. The Old Testament records God revealing Himself to men and women through many means, while the New Testament demonstrated His power and purposes through miracles and signs. The greatest revelation, the incarnation of Jesus Christ, bifurcates history, and when He returns, Christ will bring history to an end. For the Christian, then, history is linear, has purpose and meaning, and is filled with hope.

Second, the Christian approach to history is a commitment to God's sovereignty. Daniel 4:17, 25 affirms in the message to King Nebuchadnezzar that God rules in the affairs of men, seeking the counsel of no one. The Old Testament also declares that God's sovereignty entails overruling the evil deeds of men so that His purposes are attained. The narrative of Joseph details God's providence over his life—"the Lord was with Joseph"—despite the evil intents of Potiphar's wife and of Joseph's brothers. God's purpose was to preserve life, and Joseph was His means of doing that. Furthermore, God's sovereignty extends to the counsel that rulers receive. Second Samuel 17:14 demonstrates that God thwarted the counsel of Absalom's adviser, Ahithophel, to secure the safety of David's retreat from Absalom.

The crucifixion of Jesus Christ constitutes the foremost New Testament example of God's sovereignty in the face of evil. Acts 4:27-28 depicts this monstrous evil as under God's sovereign control: "For truly in this city there were gathered together against Your holy servant Jesus, whom You anointed, both Herod and Pontius Pilate, along with the Gentiles and the peoples of Israel, to do whatever Your hand and Your purpose predestined to occur."

A third element in the Christian approach to history is that God uses pagan nations to accomplish His ends. When Jeremiah warned Judah that God was about to judge them for their spiritual adultery, he shows God summoning Nebuchadnezzar, "My servant," to be the instrument of His judgment. In Jeremiah 27:7 God declares, "all the nations shall serve him, and his son, and his grandson, until the time of his own land comes." When Isaiah prophesied of the coming liberation of the exiles from captivity, he prophetically named the Persian ruler Cyrus as the one to effect that liberation. God said of Cyrus, "He is My shepherd! And he will perform all My desire . . . Whom I have taken by the right hand, to subdue nations before him, and to loose the loins of kings" (Isa. 44:28—45:1). Thus the Bible strips away the surface of history and reveals the transcendent sovereign God moving history His way.

Finally, the Christian approach to history focuses on the principle of justice that pervades God's character and subsequently His history. When He uses a pagan nation to accomplish His ends, as He did in choosing Babylon to judge Judah, His justice demands that that nation likewise be judged. In Jeremiah 50:29 God calls for the nations to align against Babylon: "Repay her according to her work; according to all that she has done, so do to her; for she has become arrogant against the LORD, against the Holy One of Israel." When the nation God has raised up accomplishes His purposes, He judges that nation righteously and justly. Just as an individual cannot sin with impunity, the same is true for a nation.

It is rare today to approach world events with the certainty of Jeremiah revealing God's workings with Babylon and Judah, but we can gain a principle that produces confidence and certainty: God stands above the line of history as sovereign. Our assurance is that He controls all that occurs on that line for His glorious purposes. There is no geographical refuge that can guarantee such security. It comes only from faith and trust in the sovereign God of history.

Genuine biblical Christianity is a holistic worldview that provides the answers to the key questions of life. It is under severe attack today within Western civilization. Both the postmodern and the secular mindset see biblical Christianity as the only major Western worldview articulating and defending absolutes. In that sense, biblical Christianity is the enemy of pluralism and relativism. This book has offered a clear articulation of its major tenets and its distinctives in this pluralistic world. Because our Lord has commanded it and because the fate of billions depends on it, biblical Christianity must be defended with love, and it must be championed with courage and boldness.

FOR FURTHER DISCUSSION

1. Describe a time in your life when you began wrestling with one or more of the penetrating worldview questions. What was your approach to finding answers?

2. What new insights have you gleaned from this chapter about God, Jesus, or salvation?
3. In what ways does an in-depth understanding of the Christian worldview strengthen your faith?
4. Discuss what you would say to a Mormon in defense of the Trinity.
5. What characteristics of the biblical Christian worldview distinguish it from all other worldviews presented in this book?
6. What are the three major ethical points that characterize biblical Christianity? Give reasons for the superiority of the Christian ethical system.
7. How does a Christian approach to history impact your daily life?
8. What are the key learnings you will take with you from this book? How will your life and faith be different as a result of this study?

NOTES

CHAPTER 1—POSTMODERNISM

1. Jeffrey L. Sheler, "Faith in America," *US News and World Report* (May 6, 2002), 40.
2. Ibid., 42.
3. Ibid., 42-43.
4. Ibid., 43.
5. *Time* (October 13, 1997), 81.
6. Millard Erickson, *Postmodernizing the Faith* (Grand Rapids: Baker, 1998), 16-17.
7. Stanley Grenz, "Postmodernism and the Future of Evangelical Theology: *Star Trek* and the Next Generation," *Evangelical Review of Theology* 18:2 (October 1994), 325.
8. Alister McGrath, *A Passion for Truth* (Downers Grove, Ill.: InterVarsity, 1996), 186.
9. Cited by John Leo, "Professors Who See No Evil," *US News and World Report* (July 22, 2002), 14.
10. Ibid., 14.
11. Alister McGrath, *Intellectuals Don't Need God and Other Modern Myths* (Grand Rapids: Zondervan, 1993), 28.
12. Ken Boa, *Cults, World Religions and You* (Wheaton, Ill.: Victor Books, 1981), 10-14.

CHAPTER 2—NATURALISM

1. James Davison Hunter, *Culture Wars* (New York: Basic Books, 1991).
2. Cited by James P. Eckman in *Exploring Church History* (Wheaton, Ill.: Crossway Books/ETA, 2002), 72.
3. This survey of the Enlightenment is taken from ibid., 71-74.
4. Ibid., 93-94.
5. Ian S. Markham, ed., *A World Religions Reader*, 2nd ed. (Malden, Mass.: Blackwell, 2000), 240.
6. Paul Kurtz, ed., *The Humanist Manifesto I and II* (Buffalo: Prometheus Books, 1973), 8.
7. Quoted in James Sire, *The Universe Next Door: A Basic Worldview Catalog*, 3rd ed. (Downers Grove, Ill.: InterVarsity, 1997), 63.
8. Ibid., 65-66.
9. Paul Kurtz, ed., *The Humanist Manifesto I and II* (Buffalo: Prometheus Books, 1973), 16.
10. Ibid., 17.

11. Ibid.
12. See Fritz Ridenour, *So What's the Difference?* (Glendale, Calif.: Regal Books, 1967), 118-29.
13. Kurtz, *Humanist Manifesto I and II*, 17.

CHAPTER 3—HINDUISM

1. Percival Spear, *India, Pakistan, and the West* (Oxford: Oxford University Press, 1958), 57.
2. This summary of the Hindu texts is taken from Arthur J. Dalavai, "A Critical Appraisal of and Christian Approach to Philosophical Hinduism," Th.D. dissertation (Dallas Theological Seminary, 1977), 85-103.
3. This survey of Hindu history is taken from Geoffrey Parrinder, ed., *World Religions: From Ancient History to the Present* (Bicester, England: Hamlyn, 1971), 192-238 and John B. Noss, *Man's Religions*, 6th ed. (New York: Macmillan, 1980), 72-94, 177-219.
4. Upanishads, I, 34.
5. Taken from Michael J. Longden, "Some Prominent Doctrines of Divinity, Man, and Salvation in Hinduism," Unpublished Master's thesis (Dallas Theological Seminary, 1974), 46.
6. Malcolm Pitt, *Introducing Hinduism* (New York: Friendship Press, 1955), 21.
7. These definitions were drawn from Noss's book, *Man's Religions*, 88-92.
8. Sir Norman Anderson, ed., *The World's Religions* (Grand Rapids: Eerdmans, 1950), 148.
9. This explanation of reincarnation is based on Robert A. Morey, *Reincarnation and Christianity* (Minneapolis: Bethany Fellowship, 1980), 11-21.
10. This review of the bridges and barriers to Hinduism comes from Dalavai, "A Critical Appraisal of and Christian Approach to Philosophical Hinduism," 125-37.

CHAPTER 4—BUDDHISM

1. Richard A. Gard, *Buddhism* (Englewood Cliffs, N. J.: Prentice-Hall, 1961), 13.
2. David Bentley Taylor, "Buddhism," in *The World's Religions*, ed. Sir Norman Anderson (Grand Rapids: Eerdmans, 1950), 178.
3. Richard Robinson and Willard Johnson, *The Buddhist Religion* (Belmont, Calif.: Dickinson), 14.
4. John B. Noss, *Man's Religions*, 6th ed. (New York: Macmillan, 1980), 106-09.
5. Ibid., 109-10.
6. W. St. Clair-Tisdall, *The Noble Eightfold Path* (London: Elliot Stock, 1903), 181.
7. Fritz Ridenour, *So What's the Difference?* (Glendale, Calif.: Regal, 1967), 106-09; Noss, *Man's Religions*, 175.
8. Noss, *Man's Religions*, 113; Subhadra Bhikshu, *A Buddhist Catechism* (London: George Redway, 1890), 43-45.
9. Ridenour, *So What's the Difference?* 109-10.

10. This summary of the two sects of Buddhism is based on Ridenour, *So What's the Difference?* 110-11.
11. Noss, *Man's Religions,* 114-15.
12. Ibid., 118.
13. Ibid., 122.
14. Bhikshu, *A Buddhist Catechism,* 35.
15. Ibid., 58-59.

CHAPTER 5—CONFUCIANISM

1. Lin Yutang, ed., *The Wisdom of Confucius* (New York: Random House, 1938), 5.
2. John B. Noss, *Man's Religions,* 6th ed. (New York: Macmillan, 1980), 266-68.
3. Laurence G. Thompson, *Chinese Religion: An Introduction,* 2nd ed. (Encino, Calif.: Dickerson, 1975), 6.
4. Ibid., 5.
5. Ian S. Markham, ed., *A World Religions Reader,* 2nd ed. (Malden, Mass.: Blackwell, 2000), 160.
6. Thompson, *Chinese Religion: An Introduction,* 19.
7. See Noss, *Man's Religions,* 269-70.
8. Ibid., 278.
9. Ibid., 271.
10. James Legge, *Confucian Analects* (Oxford: Oxford University Press, 1892), VI:28.
11. Enoch Wan, "The Confucian Ethic and the Chinese Cultural Attitudes Toward Work," *Crux* 24:3 (September 1988), 2.
12. James Hastings, ed., *The Encyclopedia of Religion and Ethics* (New York: Scribner's, 1965), 16.
13. Noss, *Man's Religions,* 279.
14. Ibid.
15. Ibid., 296-300.
16. Markham, *A World Religions Reader,* 187.

CHAPTER 6—SHINTOISM

1. Ian Buruma, "After Hirohito," *The New York Times Magazine* (May 28, 1989), 29, 52-57.
2. Ian S. Markham, ed., *A World Religions Reader,* 2nd ed. (Malden, Mass.: Blackwell, 2000), 201.
3. John B. Noss, *Man's Religions,* 6th ed. (New York: Macmillan, 1980), 302-03.
4. Ibid., 304; Joseph M. Kitagawa, *Religion in Japanese History* (New York: Columbia, 1966), 28, 34, 38.
5. Noss, *Man's Religions,* 304-05; Kitagawa, *Religion in Japanese History,* 30.
6. Kitagawa, *Religion in Japanese History,* 34, 38, 57-59; Noss, *Man's Religions,* 161-63.
7. Noss, *Man's Religions,* 311-12.

8. Clark Offner, "Shinto," in *The World's Religions*, ed. Sir Norman Anderson (Grand Rapids: Eerdmans, 1950), 192, 312, 321, 325.

9. Ibid., 193-94.

10. Noss, *Man's Religions*, 305-06.

11. Offner, "Shinto," 198-99.

12. Ibid., 199-200.

CHAPTER 7—JUDAISM

1. Marvin R. Wilson, "A History of Contempt," *Christianity Today* (October 7, 1988), 60.

2. Ibid., 61-65.

3. See John B. Noss, *Man's Religions*, 6th ed. (New York: Macmillan, 1980), 391-94.

4. Sir Norman Anderson, ed., *The World's Religions* (Grand Rapids: Eerdmans, 1950), 55.

5. Authorized Prayer Book, 56-57.

6. Fritz Ridenour, *So What's the Difference?* (Glendale, Calif.: Regal, 1967), 71-72.

7. Ibid., 72-73.

8. Anderson, *The World's Religions*, 63-64.

9. Ibid., 74; Ridenour, *So What's the Difference?* 73.

10. Anderson, *The World's Religions*, 67.

11. Ibid., 63.

12. Thomas Friedman, *From Beirut to Jerusalem* (New York: Doubleday, 1989).

13. Ibid., 285-87.

14. Ridenour, *So What's the Difference?* 78.

CHAPTER 8—ISLAM

1. For this historical review, see James A. Beverley, "Muhammad amid the Faiths," *Christian History* (22:2), 10-15 and "Islam: A Christian Perspective," a pamphlet of InterAct Ministries, n.d.

2. Beverley, "Muhammad amid the Faiths," 13.

3. Patrick O. Cate, *Understanding and Responding to Islam* (Dallas: Dallas Theological Seminary, 2001), 12-14.

4. Qur'an, 11:52.

5. Ibid., 5:72.73.

6. Ibid., 3:78.

7. Ibid., 5:48.

8. Ibid., 5:52.

9. For this survey of the teaching of Islam, see George Fry and James King, *A Survey of the Muslim Faith* (Grand Rapids: Baker, 1979), 40-65.

10. This review of the pillars is summarized in Beverley, "Muhammad amid the Faiths," 14-15.

11. See Mateen A. Elass, "Four Jihads," *Christian History* (21:2), 35-38.

12. This section has summarized the entire book by Charles R. Marsh, *Share Your Faith with a Muslim* (Chicago: Moody, 1975).

CHAPTER 9—THE NEW AGE MOVEMENT

1. Shirley MacLaine, *It's All in the Playing* (New York: Bantam, 1987), 191-93.
2. Edmund C. Gruss, *Cults and the Occult* (Phillipsburg, N.J.: Presbyterian and Reformed, 1994), 204-06.
3. James Sire, *The Universe Next Door: A Basic Worldview Catalog* (Downers Grove, Ill.: InterVarsity, 1988), 165-67.
4. Gruss, *Cults and the Occult*, 205.
5. Douglas Groothius, *Unmasking the New Age* (Downers Grove, Ill.: InterVarsity, 1986), 77-78.
6. Sire, *The Universe Next Door*, 161-65.
7. Ibid., 170-71.
8. Shirley MacLaine, *Dancing in the Light* (New York: Bantam, 1985), 309.
9 Sire, *The Universe Next Door*, 178.
10. Gruss, *Cults and the Occult*, 208.
11. Shirley MacLaine, *Out on a Limb* (New York: Bantam, 1983), 140-50.
12. Groothius, *Unmasking the New Age*, 20-31; Gruss, *Cults and the Occult*, 208-10.
13. Randall Baer, *Inside the New Age Nightmare* (Lafayette, La.: Huntington, 1989), 186 and Gruss, *Cults and the Occult*, 211.
14. See Sire, *The Universe Next Door*, 203.
15. Ibid., 204.
16. Ibid., 207.

CHAPTER 10—THE JEHOVAH'S WITNESS, CHRISTIAN SCIENCE, AND MORMON WORLDVIEWS

1. Anthony Hoekema, *The Four Major Cults* (Grand Rapids: Eerdmans, 1963), 378-403.
2. Ken Boa, *Cults, World Religions and You* (Wheaton, Ill.: Victor Books, 1981), 77-78.
3. Edmond C. Gruss, *Cults and the Occult* (Phillipsburg, N.J.: Presbyterian and Reformed, 1994), 17 and Hoekema, *The Four Major Cults*, 238-39.
4. For this historical summary, see Boa, *Cults, World Religions, and You*, 81-84.
5. Ibid., 84.
6. Ibid.
7. Gruss, *Cults and the Occult*, 57-58.
8. For this summary of Mormon history, see Boa, *Cults, World Religions, and You*, 64-68 and Gruss, *Cults and the Occult*, 29-37.
9. Boa, *Cults, World Religions, and You*, 67-68.
10. Ibid., 68.
11. *Time* (August 4, 1997), 54.

12. Boa, *Cults, World Religions, and You*, 84.
13. This section on cult theology was based on the chart titled "Christianity, Cults, and Religions" (Torrance, Calif.: Rose Publishing, 1994); Boa, *Cults, World Religions, and You*, 64-89; Gruss, *Cults and the Occult*, 12-65; Walter Martin, *The Kingdom of the Cults* (Minneapolis: Bethany Fellowship, 1977), 34-198.
14. See Ronald Enroth, "How Can You Reach a Cultist?" *Moody Monthly* (November 1987), 66-68.

CHAPTER 11—ROMAN CATHOLICISM, PROTESTANTISM, AND EASTERN ORTHODOXY: WHAT'S THE DIFFERENCE?

1. This summary of Catholicism is taken from James P. Eckman, *Exploring Church History* (Wheaton, Ill.: Crossway Books/ETA, 2002), 17-47.
2. For this historical survey see Daniel B. Clendenin, *Eastern Orthodox Christianity: A Western Perspective* (Grand Rapids: Baker, 1994), 454-55.
3. For this historic review of Protestantism, see Eckman, *Exploring Church History*, 49-57, 83-99.
4. Joseph Cardinal Ratzinger, *Catechism of the Catholic Church* (Liguori, Mo.: Liguori Press, 1994), 26.
5. Ibid., 251-52, 254.
6. Ibid., 312-25, 334-56.
7. Ibid., 288-92 and Fritz Ridenour, *So What's the Difference?* (Glendale, Calif.: Regal, 1967), 39-51.
8. Daniel Clendenin, "Why I'm Not Orthodox," *Christianity Today* (January 6, 1997), 35.
9. Ibid., 36-37.
10. Ibid., 120.
11. Ibid., 130.
12. Ibid., 131.
13. Ibid., 106-07.
14. Ibid., 107-08.

CHAPTER 12—CHRISTIANITY AS A WORLDVIEW

1. James W. Sire, *The Universe Next Door: A Basic Worldview Catalog* (Downers Grove, Ill.: InterVarsity, 1988), 17-18.
2. See James P. Eckman, *Exploring Church History* (Wheaton, Ill.: Crossway Books/ETA, 2002), 30-32.
3. Ibid., 32-35.
4. Erwin Lutzer, *The Necessity of Ethical Absolutes* (Dallas: Probe, 1981), 70.
5. This review of ethics is taken from James P. Eckman, *Biblical Ethics: Choosing Right in a World Gone Wrong* (Wheaton, Ill.: Crossway Books/ETA, 2004), 16-18.

Bibliography

Dockery, David S. *The Challenge of Postmodernism: An Evangelical Engagement.* Wheaton, Ill.: BridgePoint, 1995.

Naugle, David K. *Worldview: The History of a Concept.* Grand Rapids: Eerdmans, 2002.

Sire, James W. *The Universe Next Door: A Basic Worldview Catalog,* 3rd ed. Downers Grove, Ill.: InterVarsity, 1997.

Veith, Gene Edward, Jr. *Postmodern Times: A Christian Guide to Contemporary Thought and Culture.* Wheaton, Ill.: Crossway Books, 1994.

WORLD RELIGIONS

Anderson, Sir Norman. *Christianity and World Religions.* Downers Grove, Ill.: InterVarsity, 1984. (Updated version of 1950 book.)

_____. *The World's Religions.* Grand Rapids: Eerdmans, 1950.

Boa, Kenneth. *Cults, World Religions and You.* Wheaton, Ill.: Victor Books, 1981.

Clendenin, Daniel B. *Eastern Orthodox Christianity: A Western Perspective.* Grand Rapids: Baker, 1994.

_____, ed. *Eastern Orthodox Theology: A Contemporary Reader.* Grand Rapids: Baker, 1995.

Markham, Ian S., ed. *A World Religions Reader,* 2nd ed. Oxford and Malden, Mass.: Blackwell, 2000.

Moucarry, Chawkat. *The Prophet and the Messiah: An Arab Christian's Perspective on Islam and Christianity.* Downers Grove, Ill.: InterVarsity, 2001.

Noss, John B. *Man's Religions.* 6th Edition. New York: Macmillan, 1980.

Parrinder, Geoffrey, ed. *World Religions from Ancient History to the Present.* Bicester, England: Hamlyn, 1971.

Ratzinger, Joseph Cardinal. *Catechism of the Catholic Church.* Liguori, Mo.: Liguori Press, 1994.

Zacharias, Ravi. *Jesus Among Other Gods.* Nashville: Nelson, 2000.

CULTS

Berry, Harold J. *Truth Twisters.* Lincoln, Neb.: Back to the Bible, 1987.

Gruss, Edmond C. *Cults and the Occult.* Phillipsburg, N.J.: Presbyterian and Reformed, 1994.

Martin, Walter R. *The Kingdom of the Cults.* Minneapolis: Bethany Fellowship, 1977.

Ridenour, Fritz. *So What's the Difference?* Glendale, Calif.: Regal, 1967.

OTHER RESOURCES

Lewis, C. S. *The Problem of Pain.* New York: Macmillan, 1962.

Yancey, Philip. *Where Is God When It Hurts?* Grand Rapids: Zondervan, 1977.

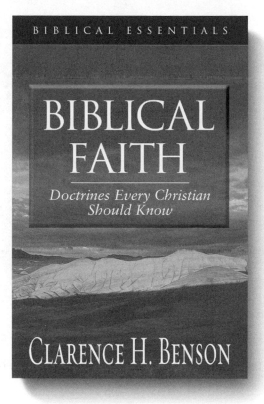

BIBLICAL FAITH:
DOCTRINES EVERY CHRISTIAN SHOULD KNOW
CLARENCE H. BENSON

Why do Christians study doctrine? You might say our faith depends on it. In a culture that promotes a variety of religions and argues that all are equally valid, it is essential that Christians know doctrine. Without sound doctrine, our faith is in danger of being distorted or destroyed. In *Biblical Faith,* Dr. Benson offers a concise, straightforward explanation of twelve basic doctrines. The book begins by discussing what evangelical Christians believe about Scripture and then explores doctrines from Creation and the Fall to heaven and hell. The most profound truths of the Bible are described in a way that is clear and easy to understand.

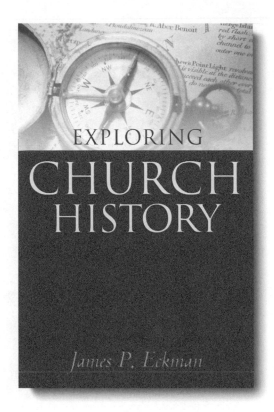

EXPLORING CHURCH HISTORY
JAMES P. ECKMAN

When we study church history, we are learning about more than just names and dates. We are exploring our own Christian heritage. And as we study the past, we also prepare ourselves for the future, because many contemporary issues are not new at all. A study of church history also gives an accurate understanding of the complexities and richness of Christianity. The church has suffered much, but a thorough look at its past reinforces our conviction that the church will triumph. Dr. James Eckman leads readers through church history from the Pentecost to the present. This basic introduction, done chronologically, emphasizes the theological process and developing consensus within the church on what the Scriptures teach, as well as the institutional development of the church.

EXPLORING THE OLD TESTAMENT
SAMUEL J. SCHULTZ AND GARY V. SMITH

It is imperative for every growing Christian to study all of the Bible. In *Exploring the Old Testament*, Samuel Schultz and Gary Smith survey the content of the Old Testament so that readers will understand each book's events and themes. Chapters conclude with projects, questions, and exploration activities that not only test readers' grasp of the materials but also provide opportunity for more detailed and intensive study. This book acquaints people with the Old Testament's major divisions and its amazing unity as a whole. Both authors are well-equipped to guide readers through the Old Testament. Schultz is Professor Emeritus of Bible and Theology at Wheaton Graduate School, and Smith is Professor of Old Testament at Midwestern Baptist Theological Seminary.

EXPLORING THE NEW TESTAMENT
WALTER M. DUNNETT

Exploring the New Testament takes a survey approach that will deepen your knowledge of God and enrich your understanding of the Bible. Readers will gain an overview of the entire New Testament, consider the respective writers and their work, and understand the purpose, outline, main content, and leading features of each New Testament book. All of these elements lay a solid foundation for understanding the message and revelation of Jesus Christ. The chapters end with application activities and discussion questions. Author Walter Dunnett served on the faculty of Northwestern College.

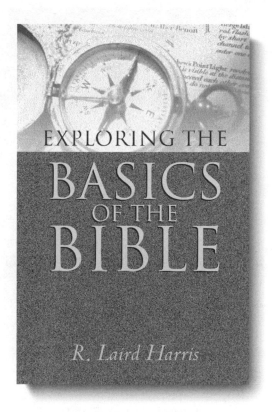

EXPLORING THE BASICS OF THE BIBLE
R. LAIRD HARRIS

The Scriptures are God's Word to us. We should personally read them, study them, meditate upon them, and most of all, practice them. But the first step to a truly enriching study of the Bible is understanding the basics behind its writing. R. Laird Harris's introductory book explores important questions that many wonder about: Who wrote the Bible? How was it written? Why should I believe that it is God's Word? What about its seeming contradictions and problems? All these topics and more are covered in this thorough treatment of the truth about the Bible. The book concludes with chapters on study helps and Bible study methods, as well as a list of resources for enrichment. Harris is widely known and respected for his biblical scholarship, as well as his past teaching and leadership at Covenant Theological Seminary.

EVIDENCE AND TRUTH:
FOUNDATIONS FOR CHRISTIAN TRUTH
ROBERT J. MORGAN

How do we know that Christianity is true? How do we respond to doubters who say that our faith is only about fictional stories and unfounded feelings? In *Evidence and Truth,* Robert Morgan takes readers step-by-step through the well-documented historical and physical evidence that supports the claims of Christianity. He deals with such topics as the resurrection of Christ, the complexity of creation, the reliability of the Bible, and the changed lives of believers. Whether the reader is looking for personal answers or wants to be prepared to answer a friend, this book will help. *Evidence and Truth* offers a solid intellectual basis from which the reader can take a step of faith and experience the ultimate assurance that comes from God's Spirit. A graduate of Columbia International University and Wheaton College Graduate School, Morgan pastored for nearly twenty-five years and has authored several books.

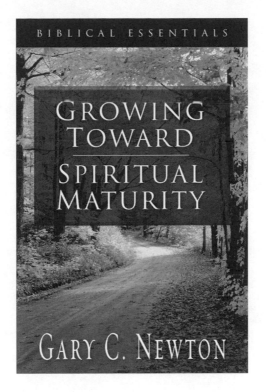

GROWING TOWARD SPIRITUAL MATURITY
GARY C. NEWTON

Spiritual growth is a journey, a lifelong process. And it is not something that we can do on our own; true spiritual growth occurs only when we invite the Holy Spirit into our lives to change us from the inside out. This concise study by Gary C. Newton offers a practical strategy for growing toward Christlikeness using all the resources God has provided us—His Word, the Church, the ability to meet with Him in prayer, and others—under the illumination of the Holy Spirit. Spiritual disciplines such as Bible study, prayer, a godly lifestyle, witnessing, and using spiritual gifts are explained and explored.

Since 1930
Evangelical Training Association

THE MINISTRIES OF EVANGELICAL TRAINING ASSOCIATION

(ETA)

Experienced – Founded in 1930.
Doctrinally Dependable – Conservative and evangelical theology.
Educationally Sound – Engaging all adult learning styles.
Thoroughly Field-Tested – Used by a global constituency.
Recommended – Officially endorsed by denominations and schools.
Ministry Driven – Committed to quality training resources for equipping lay volunteers to serve Christ more effectively in the church.
Affordable – Attractive and reasonably priced.

For many local ministries, the most important step to an effective lay leadership training program is locating and implementing an inspiring, motivational system of instruction. ETA curriculum is available as traditional classroom courses, audio and video seminars, audio and video CD-ROM packages, and other resources for your classroom teaching or personal study.

Contact ETA today for free information and a 20-minute video presentation. Request Information Packet: Crossway Partner.

EVANGELICAL TRAINING ASSOCIATION
110 Bridge Street • PO Box 327 • Wheaton, IL 60189
800-369-8291 • FAX 630-668-8437 • www.etaworld.org